A   LEGACY

A LEGACY

His Life

His Works

His Missions

His Monuments

By

Charles W. Polzer, S.J.

Jesuit Fathers of Southern Arizona

Tucson   Arizona
1998

Padre Eusebio Francisco Kino

In 1964 the Padre Kino Memorial Statue Committee commissioned Frances O'Brien of Tucson, Arizona, to compose a portrait of Eusebio Francisco Kino that would depict the "Pioneer
Padre" as historically accurate as humanly possible. Having
studied dozens of photos of family descendents, she first made a
soft pencil sketch and later painted his portrait in oil. The
picture on the opposite page is a reproduction of the pencil sketch;
the oil painting is preserved at the Arizona Historical Society,
Tucson, Arizona.

Library of Congress Catalog Card Number
LC97-92849

ISBN 0-9661562-0-X

DEDICATION

To Jane Harrison Ivancovich

A timeless friend to historians, a devotee of quality publication, a sponsor of innovative scholarship, and a staunch advocate of preservation, Jane came to the Southwest from her native Ohio with hopes to bolster her health. She found that the wonders of the desert suited her body and soul. Those who had the privilege of knowing her recognized in her a woman of high intelligence, sensitive artistry, and uncompromising principle. Yet, she was always humorous, humble, and thoroughly human.

Jane had a natural affinity for Padre Kino because she studied in Italy, raised horses, and loved the desert. So when she encountered the celebratory events of 1961 regarding Kino, she was at home among erudite scholars, helping to humanize their perceptions of the pioneer padre. Among them the renowned British historian James Broderick, S.J. held her in such high esteem he dedicated his last work on Galileo to her.

This writer, too, owes her much. Her insistence brought me to Tucson; her encouragement was instrumental in founding the Southwestern Mission Research Center on which board we served for nearly twenty years. She championed the incorporation of Amerisearch, unselfishly supported the Documentary Relations of the Southwest at the Arizona State Museum, and quietly sponsored many activities of the American Division of the Jesuit Historical Institute, housed at the Arizona State Museum.

Her interest and support for things involving Jesuits and Padre Kino rank her with the Duchess of Aveiro. Among us she was always "La Doña Juana."

ACKNOWLEDGEMENTS

This book, *KINO: A Legacy*, has evolved through nearly thirty years of research and writing about Jesuits and Jesuit missions in northern Mexico. Many readers will recognize some time-honored phrases and a few treasured photos. For the most part, however, this book is a thorough re-working of the old *Kino Guide II* that accompanied thousands of visitors to the Pimería Alta.

One recurring debt of gratitude is to the Southwestern Mission Research Center for years of trust and support. Since my separation from the SMRC and their change in publication philosophy, new sources of support have come from Amerisearch, Inc. and from the Southwest Foundation. Their generous awards, in the continuing spirit of Jane Harrison Ivancovich, have made this book possible

The original *Kino Guide* (1968) was painstakingly handled by Arizona Lithographers. Then over the years and a succession of owner/printers, the newer editions rolled off the presses of the same shop. This edition is no different due to the guidance of John Davis and his professional staff. Through John I learned of Ray Harden who is responsible for the fine maps in this volume and for the cover design. Sharon Nicks of Types sheperded me through the staggering world of digitization. Great friends like Don Bufkin, Tom Naylor, and James Officer have long since joined Padre Kino on the trail. They did much for the things this book contains, and I hope their spirits shine forth in what has been set in photo and type.

Charles W. Polzer, S.J.

About the Author

Charles William Polzer was born in San Diego, California, in 1930 and graduated from St. Augustine's High School. He received his first Bachelor's degree in Political Science from Santa Clara University in 1952 at which time he entered the California Province of the Society of Jesus. Pursuing the normal course of Jesuit studies, he received degrees in Government and Philosophy at St. Louis University, Missouri, in 1960. Then, he taught three years at Brophy College Preparatory in Phoenix, Arizona, where he began to immerse himself in regional history. Following his ordination to the priesthood in June, 1964, he finished theological studies at Alma College and made his tertianship in Córdoba, Spain, returning to the United States in 1966.

Accepted into the doctoral program in History and Anthropology at the University of Arizona in 1966, he received the Ph.D. in 1972. He joined the faculty of the University as an ethnohistorian in the Arizona State Museum where he is currently a curator. In 1985 he was appointed to the Christopher Columbus Quincentenary Jubilee Commission created by Congress in the previous year. He served until its dissolution in 1993. King Juan Carlos of Spain conferred on him the Order of Isabela La Católica in1987 for his distinguished work in the history of the Americas. He actively directs the American Division of the Jesuit Historical Institute based in Tucson, Arizona.

Jesuit Fathers of Southern Arizona

The Jesuit Fathers of Southern Arizona was incorporated in Arizona in 1969 to stabilize the activities of the California Province of the Society in the southern sector of the state. This publication has been undertaken by them to insure continuity for study in the history of the Society of Jesus in the region. They are also responsible in overseeing local activities in regard to the beatification of Padre Kino, an ecclesiastical process now nearing completion.

CONTENTS

X

EUSEBIO FRANCISCO KINO, S.J.
PIONEER PADRE OF THE PIMERÍA ALTA

The desert appears lifeless, deserted, void. Its arid mountains are etched in emptiness by the strong shadows of the parching sun. Mesas of mesquite and cactus are ripped apart by bouldered arroyos. Stillness covers its sun baked horizons. To each generation the desert seems history-less and hostile. It is no place for man, much less his dreams.

This is how the desert appears to one who has never probed its realities, for the desert is alive and has been filled with the dreams of men who have made history here. The desert is a paradox. For centuries it has been a home for strong men, for men of faith and vision. The desert is a place where life takes on greater meaning because it survives in an environment of natural extremes. The desert is a paradox of life itself.

This is the story of a man who understood that paradox of the desert – Eusebio Francisco Kino, priest and missionary to the Pimería Alta. He spent his life among less educated desert peoples, turning river banks into farms, dirt into dwellings and churches, and dreams into living realities. He respected this land and matched its strengths. Padre Kino wrote into the sands of the southwestern deserts a history as strongly etched in time as the mountains that witnessed his work.

Many men have come to the desert and made history – Cabeza de Vaca, Vásquez de Coronado, Juan de Oñate, Juan Bautista de Anza, and Francisco Garcés, but none have equaled the record of this dedicated Jesuit missionary. His vision reached beyond the thirsting horizon and his influence has spanned centuries, so well did he know the desert land and its people.

When Padre Kino arrived on the "Rim of Christendom" in 1687, he was already an experienced missionary although a newcomer to northern New Spain. His assignment to the frontier of the Pimería Alta, the land of the Upper Piman Indians, had been another unforeseen development in a life long series of circumstances that seemed like continued reversals. But nothing ever dampened his enthusiasm or dimmed his dreams.

1

THE EARLY YEARS IN EUROPE

The saga of Padre Kino begins in Segno, a tiny mountain town in the Italian Tyrol, not far from historic Trent. There on August 10, 1645, Eusebio was born in a typical stone and timber house similar to those that stud the slopes of the Dolomite Alps along the Val di Non. He was the only son of Franceso Chini and Margherita Lucchi and the brother of three sisters, Margherita, Catarina, and Ana María. His boyhood in Segno shaped the powerful frame that would one day explore the mountains and deserts of a land a hemisphere away. He learned the essentials of life on the family farm at Moncou which was later sold after his father's death in 1660; the sale included the home, buildings, vineyards, and livestock. So Eusebio was not unfamiliar with agriculture from the earliest days of his childhood.

1645

1660

Young Eusebio must have shown some degree of brilliance because his parents provided him with a private tutor, Giorgio Coradinus Mollari, and then sent him off to the newly founded Jesuit *gymnasio* at Trent where he was introduced to the world of science and letters. Three years after his father's death, the family holdings at Moncou were sold to liquidate some debts and finance Eusebio's education at the college of Hall near Innsbruck in Austria. He registered in the program of rhetoric and logic, moving on to Friburg in 1664. While studying at Hall, Kino contracted an unidentified illness that brought him close to death. These were obviously very emotional times for the young man from Segno who found his future confronted by serious choices. Was he destined to return to the Val di Non? His father had died when Eusebio was only fifteen; and the properties were sold to pay for his education. Or was he meant to be a missionary? Always in the back of Eusebio's mind lingered the memory of the visit of his cousin, Father Martino Martini, an accomplished China missionary; his brief visit had sparked an abiding interest in science and mathematics, almost prerequisites to be a missionary to the mysterious Orient. The sickness drew from Kino one of his deep-down dreams – for he vowed that if his patron, St. Francis Xavier, would intercede for his recovery, he would enter the Society of Jesus. His health returned and for the rest of his life Eusebio Kino valued his healing as a gift from God through the intercession of Xavier. Whatever may be said

1664

of Kino's recovery, his life was certainly to be a welcome gift for the "abandoned souls" of Baja California and the Pimería Alta.

KINO ENTERS THE SOCIETY OF JESUS

Now twenty years old, Kino set foot on the long trail of Jesuit training typical of the men of the "Company of Jesus." Entering the novitiate at Landsberg, he pronounced his first vows in 1667 when he renounced any inheritance from his family. Kino now entered on the Society's intensive course of studies at Ingolstadt, beginning with philosophy which he finished at the newly opened University of Innsbruck. Minor orders were conferred in April, 1669, and he was now ready for his first apostolic assignment, teaching basic grammar at Hall.

1667

1669

Five years had passed since his entry into the Society, but he had not forgotten his promise to volunteer for the missions; he filed his first formal petition to go to the Americas, to China, or any other difficult foreign assignment. Father General Oliva honored the offer with silence. Two of his Swiss professors, Amhryn in philosophy and Aigenler in mathematics, were named for the China missions, and this prompted Kino to appeal a second time for a similar assignment in 1672; he was being patient but insistent. After three years of "regency," the period Jesuits spend prior to theological studies, Kino again renewed his appeal to be sent to the missions. The only response from the General was a recognition of his constancy in discerning his vocation. Two more years elapsed while Kino devoted himself intensely to the study of theology and

1672

Kino Family Home in Segno, Trento, Italy

mathematics; again, he petitioned Rome. Ordination was not far off. Where would he be destined afterwards? Yet another appeal rumbled down to Father General a year later. Eusebio was showing strong determination. He was ordained a priest on June 12, 1677, at Eistady, Austria, with the other members of his class. But still, no word from Rome.

1677

The Ingolstadt years were intense ones. Not only had Kino dedicated himself to the demands of theological studies, he delved into mathematics, geography, and cartography under a faculty of distinguished professors. The Jesuits were not isolated from other students at the relatively young university, and Kino moderated a mathematics club that concentrated in the emerging field of astronomy. In fact, he converted one of the classic towers of the university building into a mini-observatory! Although the facts are scanty, one can feel the energy and enthusiasm of this determined young man from the Tyrol; the whole world and the heavens were fair game for all his talents.

The Duke of Bavaria, whose son Kino was teaching, was so impressed with his accomplishments, he invited the young priest to stay on to teach science and mathematics. Kino, as appreciative as he must have been, however, continued to press Rome for an assignment to the missions. Finishing the "tertianship" (or final probationary period in the Society's long training) at Oettingen, he knew men were being chosen for the Americas. For the sixth time, he offered himself if Father General felt that this was truly God's will for him in life and in the Society.

AMERICA OR THE ORIENT?

In late March, 1678, Kino's provincial superior arrived at the tertianship with the General's decision; he was to be assigned to the missions of the Spanish empire! Would that mean the Americas or the Orient? Neither of the two classmates now destined for the missions lost any time. On March 30, Kino and Anthony Kerschpamer left for Munich to spend a week in making preparations for the long journey. Always resourceful, special permission was granted Kino to offset travel expenses with money he had earned from the sale of scientific instruments he had been making.

Winter was wearing away as Kino and Kerschpamer rode off to Hall where the dreams of distant worlds once dominated their lives. This time, however, the dreams had become awesome realities as they bade farewell to old companions and loyal students. Threading the Brenner Pass, the two America-bound Jesuits rode through Trentino valleys and Tyrolean hills seeking family, friends, and old professors. Spring was in the air. The sun of the southern Alpine slopes beckoned new leaves and

1678

melted the edges of snow banks into rivulets of crystal water. There was life and freshness everywhere. There was hope and adventure in his voice as Kino said goodbye to childhood haunts. The Val di Non, Mezzacorona, Moncou; his sisters, uncles, and scores of relatives in the Alto Adige were swallowed up in a wake of twisting canyons and sprawling vineyards. The Tyrol now would be only a cherished memory.

Nineteen Jesuit companions converged on Genoa to begin their missionary careers. Germans, Austrians, Bohemians, Italians, and Tyrolese made up the contingent that would eventually disperse across America, the Pacific, and Asia. Who could really describe their sentiments as they set sail for Cádiz. Excitement, a raging summer thunder storm, and choppy seas worked their unwelcome magic on Kino's first time aboard an ocean-going vessel; but he was fine after a day. The *Capitana* and the *San Nicolás* under command of Francesco Colón of Genoa, tacked on toward the Spanish peninsula. Eight days out of Genoa, as Minorca slid past the horizon, huge sails were bearing down on the course of the two Italian ships. General quarters were sounded to prepare the one armed ship to give battle to Turkish pirates. But as the men-of-war approached, a saludatory salvo rang out; they were, for now, a friendly English squadron!

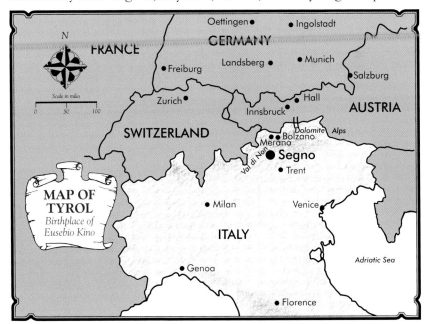

The breast-works made from mattresses and boxes were stored again and the ships steered for Alicante. Nonetheless, sails continued to jab up from the horizon and battle stations were resumed off and on for the next five days until more English ships brought news that the Turks had been driven to Argel.

What a curious way the missioners must have thought to begin a life of service to the non-believer! Landing at Alicante, the Jesuits were hosted by the college because there was some thought of continuing the journey overland. Word arrived, however, that the armada was delayed at Cádiz and would not embark until around the 12th of July. The decision was taken to continue on by sea. From the 26th of June to the 14th of July the small squadron plied the stormy waters of the western Mediterranean. Phantom ships loomed up from the African coast; dense fogs confused the pilots who promptly steered the crafts into Ceuta instead of Cádiz. Then, at the crack of dawn huge sails bore down on them from the east; rushing to battle stations, again, the small Italian vessels slowly tacked away until the threatening ship vanished from sight.

By noon of the 14th they sighted the Straits of Gibraltar, falling on their knees in gratitude for having reached the classic portal to the Atlantic. The ships triumphantly scudded along the desolate coast of Trafalgar. Hope was high until sunset. Then, the brilliant sun outlined the imperial Spanish armada, standing out to sea en route to America. Kino's heart, everyone's heart sank with that setting sun. Contrary winds were keeping them from their rendezvous. Beautiful and dramatic, the sight of forty-four galleons just miles away dashed the expectations of everyone aboard! Winds, tempestuous seas, pirates and fog had interrupted their fateful journey.

THE WAIT IN SPAIN

Missing the fleet was not quite like missing a scheduled transatlantic steamer. As Padre Kino and companions feared, they would have to wait nearly two years to book new passage! Few other places in 17th century Europe could offer the advantages of Andalusia which was the virtual throat of western expansion. Ships and passengers from all over the world converged on Cádiz and Sevilla with news and cargoes. So, Kino's keen interest in the Orient was honed even more sharply with news of Macao and the Marianas, and a newly struck friendship with Father Teófilo de Angelis, the appointed superior of the Pacific missions, enkindled in Eusebio a desire to join in the expedition to the Carolines. It never happened because De Angelis embarked before a change of assignment could be received from Rome. But the interlude occasioned Kino's acquaintance by correspondence with the Duchess of Aveiro, a staunch patron of Jesuit mission activity in the Orient. Not even her powerful intercession, however, was able to divert Kino from his destiny with New Spain. While he waited for word from Rome or for permission to board an America bound armada, he spent his time mastering Spanish, some Portuguese, teaching mathematics at the Jesuit colleges in Seville 1679 and Puerto Santa María, and making scientific instruments for use in the missions.

Just over a year had elapsed when the Jesuits got their chance to sail; but learning that the destination of the small fleet was first the coast of Angola to take on slaves for the Americas, the Jesuits refused to be associated with the business. More time passed in Sevilla until the Father

Spanish Frigate

Procurator booked passage for them on the *flota* which would accompany the new Viceroy to New Spain. Rushing to board the *Nazareno* in the port of Cádiz, the expectant missionaries were thrilled to be under sail – but a large ship threatened to collide with the galleon which altered course to avoid collision and slammed into a shallow sandbar, still known today as El Diamante. Winds and waves crashed over the stricken ship, and the passengers 1680 barely escaped with their lives. Viceroy Paredes' fleet left port with a few lucky missionaries destined for the

Orient and south America. Kino recovered some of his baggage and once again sailed upriver to Sevilla for another winter of waiting.

Finally, letters arrived from Rome in mid-November that tried to calm Kino's anxieties. If the opportunity arose, he could, indeed, join his German province companions to go to Nueva Granada (Colombia) or even the *reducciones* of Paraguay. It seemed to Kino that his life's destiny was still unclear. Just what was the will of God saying? Since leaving the mountain fastness of Austria, Kino had lost out on his preference for the Orient. His companion through years of preparation, Anthony Kerschpamer, had won the draw of destinations; Kino's slip of paper read "Mexico"; Kerschpamer's, "Oriente." Like a gamy trout, he had tried to escape the hook of destiny. And now in the chill of the Andalusian winter, he hoped for other climes.

Crisp and dry, the skies of southern Spain were ideal for astronomical observations. As Kino's third winter in Sevilla debuted, a brilliant comet stretched across the peninsular skies. Using instruments of their own manufacture, the Jesuits speculated on the nature and meaning of the heavenly spectacle. For Kino it was a unique event that offered an explanation for the raging pestilence in the city. He had hardly concluded his observations when word came for the lingering Jesuits to leave for Cádiz because an armada was forming to bring the Viceroy of Peru to his post. Kino would be aboard a smaller packet or mail ship that would break off at Havana for the port of Veracruz, where he arrived May 1st or 2nd after ninety-six days at sea. America at last!

INTERLUDE IN MEXICO

Undoubtedly Kino felt much at home as he climbed the mountain trails from Veracruz to Mexico City. His detailed itinerary and report of the voyage has been lost, so we will never know his thoughts and sentiments as he approached the shores of his destined future. Although there was a rumor in the wind that he might be reassigned to the Orient, or at least the Philippines, Admiral Isidro y Atondo, the Governor of Sinaloa and the Californias, needed the skills of the neo-missionary on an expedition to Baja California. Viceroy Paredes was anxious to accommodate Atondo even though the governor had risked political retribution by refusing to become embroiled in the fiasco of the Pueblo revolt in New Mexico. Aided by his high scientific profile, Kino was signed on as Rector of the mission and Royal Cartographer for the Californias. While details of his assignment were being worked out, Kino, at the request of friends, reviewed the astronomical observations of two years which he compiled in a small treatise, publishing it in Mexico in mid-October and dispatching copies to Europe for distribution. His *Exposición Astronómica* propelled him into local prominence and challenged the erudition of the Mexican savant Don Carlos Sigüenza y Góngora. Sigüenza raged in rebuttal, and Sor Juana, the renowned literateur and poet, sang in praise. In just six months Eusebio made his mark; maybe his astronomy was mediaeval, but his rhetoric was stimulating. Wise about people and whimsical

Title Page, *Exposición*, 1682

with the world's ways, Padre Kino presented the book to Don Carlos the day before he went west. Sigüenza was furious, but Kino was gone.

THE GRAND ISLANDS OF THE CALIFORNIAS

California became Kino's first missionary territory. No Spanish expedition to the forbidding peninsula had yet succeeded, although colonization had been attempted since the memorable days of Fernán Cortez. To Kino, California was a gigantic, unknown island – a possible haven for the exhausted crews of the Manila galleons. And Admiral Atondo, unsure of the extent of the entire region, hoped that Kino would be able to make an accurate survey of the coasts and the interior mountains. Kino was certain of his cartographic skills and hoped for opportunities to convert scattered tribes to Christianity. Unquestionably the purposes of crown and cross could both be served.

When Kino rode westward to join the expeditionary forces, three ships were already under construction at Nío on the Sinaloa River, just a few miles downstream from Atondo's headquarters at San Felipe (Sinaloa). Two were frigates and the third a slender sloop. Wood was floated down the river from the foothills of the Sierra Madre, but essential hardware

1682

9

had to be freighted from Mexico. Following that same route, Kino stopped over in Guadalajara to confer with Bishop Juan Garabito, whose ecclesiastical jurisdiction extended over the western "islands." There had been a furious dispute between Garabito and the Bishop of Durango, Fray Bartolomé Escañuela, because some Franciscans since mid-century had claimed jurisdiction over lands west of New Mexico! Nothing in the Spanish empire was simply done; theories abounded and paperwork cluttered up every effort, even an expedition into the unknown.

Leaving the chill of the altiplano, Padre Kino descended to the warm coastal plains and worked his way up to Nío where he found Atondo finishing the rough work on the three craft. It would still be several weeks before the ships could be floated down the winding estuary to Punto San Ignacio on the Gulf. So Kino took advantage of the time to reconfirm his appointment from Garabito. He managed a quick trip to Guadalajara to resolve the matter of jurisdiction in the Californias. By June Kino was again in the colonial settlement of El Rosario en route to Nío. With the late summer storms on the wane, it was time to launch the expeditionary fleet. So on October 28, 1682, the ships sailed south to Chacala, the seaport on the coast near Compostela. Here the final fittings were awaiting the craft, and supplies for a six month voyage were taken aboard. Once again, undaunted by the mountain escarpment, Kino rode to Guadalajara to spend the holidays with fellow Jesuits; by mid January the vessels were fully prepared for the expedition. As the moon brightened towards midnight January 17, 1683, Atondo's two frigates coasted out of the harbor, California bound. Kino had returned in ample time to embark on board the *Almiranta*, the *San Francisco Xavier*, an omen of destiny. His companion Padre Antonio Goñi was sailing with the Admiral on the *Capitana*, the *Concepción*, the larger of the two ships.

The north winds were blowing. The stubby Spanish craft gnawed their way northward losing as much as gaining with each tack. Heavier and slower, the *Concepción* fell from sight and the *San Xavier* put into Mazatlán waiting there to learn the fate of Atondo. By February 4, the two ships were rejoined in port. Having taken on wood and water, the captains decided to defy the strong Pacific winds without the *Balandra* that had lingered in Chacala, awaiting the arrival of Manuel Luque, seven skilled seamen, and Padre Antonio Suarez, the recently named

1682

1683

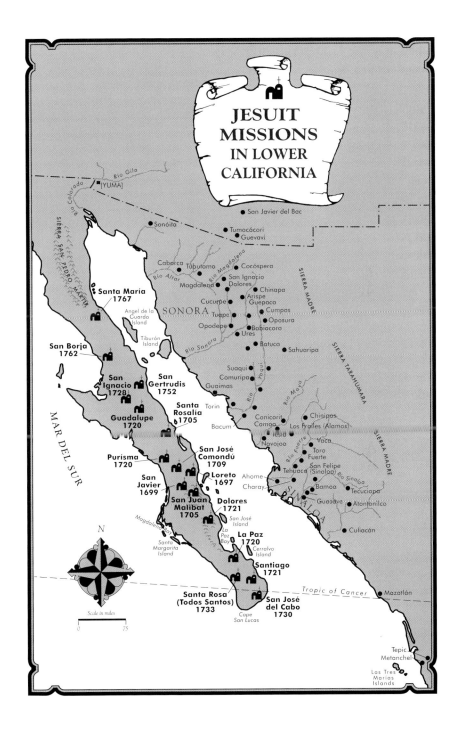

JESUIT MISSIONS IN LOWER CALIFORNIA

Rio Gila

Rio Colorado

[YUMA]

SIERRA SAN PEDRO MARTIR

San Javier del Bac

Sonóita

Tumacácori
Guevavi

Caborca
Tubutama
Cocóspera
Rio Altar
Rio Magdalena
San Ignacio
Magdalena
Dolores
Chinapa

SONORA
Cucurpe
Arispe
Guepaca

Santa María
1767
Tuape
Cumpas
Oposura

Angel de la
Guarda
Island
Opodepe
Babiacora
Ures

Tiburón
Island
Rio Sonora
Batuca
Sahuaripa

San Borja
1762
Suaqui
Comuripa
Guaimas

San
Ignacio
1728
San
Gertrudis
1752

Santa
Rosalia
1705
Torin
Conicorit
Camoa
Chinipas
Los Frailes (Alamos)

Guadalupe
1720
Bacum
Navojoa
Vaca
Toro
Fuerte

Purisma
1720
San José
Comondú
1709
Ahome
Tehueco
San Felipe
(Sinaloa)

San
Javier
1699
Loreto
1697
Charay
Bamoa
Tecuciapa

San Juan
Malibat
1705
Dolores
1721
Guasava
Atonjonilco

MAR DEL SUR
Magdalena Bay
San José
Island

Santa
Margarita
Island
La
Paz
Bay
La Paz
1720
Cerralvo
Island
Culiacán

N
Santiago
1721

Scale in miles
0   75
Santa Rosa
(Todos Santos)
1733
Cape
San Lucas
San José
del Cabo
1730
Tropic of Cancer
Mazatlán

Tepic
Metanchel

Las Tres
Marias
Islands

SIERRA MADRE

SIERRA TARAHUMARA

SIERRA MADRE

Rio Yaqui

Rio Mayo

Rio Fuerte

Rio Sinaloa

SINALOA

superior of the California missions. Atondo wondered if the sloop had passed unnoticed. Was it, perhaps, waiting for the frigates at Punto San Ignacio to make the crossing together? Both ships hoisted sail and zig-zagged against the prevailing northwesterlies; two weeks later the *San Xavier* dropped anchor at the mouth of the Sinaloa. But the *Concepción* that had been leading was no where in sight; nor was the *Balandra*. Then, two days later the flagship appeared amid cheers of relief. For the next week and half, pack trains from the neighboring missions thudded across the lowland delta laden with every conceivable item – accompanied by sheep, pigs, and chickens. There was still no word about Padre Suarez and no sight of the *Balandra*. But it was time to take advantage of favorable winds.

California at Long Last

The sun was setting over the Gulf as commands rang out to hoist the anchors and make the final move to cross the Gulf at one of its narrowest points. It was March 18. California was only hours away – except for the fact that the wind shifted and the two ships remained off shore for five days before being able to sail west. The missionaries and crew had little else to do than pray and ride the swells. A week at sea, the ships finally sighted the mountainous skyline "of the greatest island" in the

Pichilingue, La Paz

world. Both frigates slipped along the barren coast into the Bay of La Paz – it was eerie to be where Cortez had failed a century and a half before. Mexico he conquered, but California conquered him. The ships rode at anchor in view of a palm lined streamlet. Now was the time for rubrics. A steady drum roll resounded over the shallow waters of the bay. Then a crier barked out the austere proclamation of Admiral Atondo because this expedition, unlike its predecessors, would respect Indian rights and restrict blatant exploitation. Spain, and Padre Kino, had come for the conversion of the gentile tribesmen.

Launches dropped into the clear, warm water. Oars propelled them swiftly to the sandy beach, and Atondo strode to a small hilly elevation studded with palms where he proclaimed the authority of King Charles II over these new lands. The jubilant landing party thrust a huge cross into the earth and then repaired to the ships for the night. The words were done and the work commenced. The following day, April 3, launches probed the estuaries, soldiers scuffled through the sandy scrub to acquaint themselves with usable and defensible land. Only the missionaries were greatly disappointed because not a single Indian was seen anywhere.

Kino and Goñi, well aware that the solemnities of Easter were fast approaching, prepared for formal ceremonies to declare the new spiritual conquest of the Californias. Tuesday morning the 6th, the soldiers and settlers cleared the shrubbery and scattered about to cut trees for their small, half-moon fortification and for the chapel. Their work was interrupted at mid-day by a swarm of Indians brandishing bows and arrows, threatening the Spaniards and yelling for them to get out. Immediately, the soldiers picked up their muskets in defense. In the tense moments that followed neither side gave way. Then, the Spaniards gestured that they had come in peace and laid down their weapons in the hopes that the Indians would respond accordingly. No. The stand-off continued until Kino and Goñi moved forward, offering corn, biscuits, and glass beads. Adamantly refusing at first, the natives signaled for the gifts to be put on the ground. Then, they cautiously approached the missionaries and eventually took some of the proffered items from their hands. Kino probably never imagined that this would be the nature of his first contact with the people he had come to convert. In two short days of exchanges, a sense of friendliness and trust began to grow, except for the ever present bow and gun.

Day after day the Indians came to camp for more corn and hand-outs. Willingly in the context of signs and gestures, they learned to make the sign of the cross which endeared them to the religious Spaniards. It must have been a poignant experience for Padre Kino to stand on his first mission land listening to the rustle of palm branches as he contemplated the liturgy of Holy Week which would begin on the following Sunday, "Domingo de las Palmas (Ramos)." This was clearly not the Tyrol; it was a whole new beginning. As the chapel took shape, the Spaniards made their confessions and took part in the Holy Week ceremonies. Food and trinkets continued to be given to newer groups of Indians who were coming from far away. How strange it must have appeared to these rustic people to witness the complex rituals of Good Friday and the joyous release of Holy Saturday when songs rang out, muskets were fired, and bells were tolled. So went the first month in California. Truly it was the celebration of the Lord's Resurrection; new life was come to the island.

DIGGING IN FOR SURVIVAL

With the beachhead now firmly established, Atondo turned his attention to the resupply of the garrison. Hand outs of food and beads could only last a short time so the *Concepción* was replenished with wood and water for the return voyage to the mainland. It might be days, maybe months before it came back, if the initial crossing was any measure. Within weeks Atondo and the padres had opened trails across the sheer rock barrier that separated the tiny beachhead from the clusters of natives on the plateau. Their horseless expeditions encountered new groups of Indians including the Cora, who were rivals of the Guaicuros. Envy and jealousy began to infiltrate the dealings with the natives, and the portents were not comforting.

Padre Kino's kindness reached out for these plain, destitute people whose lives knew little of clothing and less of shelter. His days were filled with learning the coarse language that conveyed what meanings life held for these Guaicuro Indians. Following the norm for missionaries in new territories, both Kino and Goñi meticulously sought out and wrote down a vocabulary for the language, much of which they learned from careful

14

sign language. The good father's job was not only to befriend the Indians with the necessities of life, but to teach them the ways of civilization and even Christian doctrine, making mastery of their language essential.

As the weeks wore on, the Spaniards watched their supplies of food and trinkets diminish. Indians of both tribes became bolder in approaching the crescent shaped fortress with its fragile thatched buildings. Summer was scorching everything. Native foods were becoming scarce and the hastily planted crops were only barely gaining strength and height. Two large war parties probed the camp's defenses, but Atondo's show of force discouraged any attack. In the growing climate of fear, Zavala, a mulatto drummer boy, deserted with a band of natives. His absence was

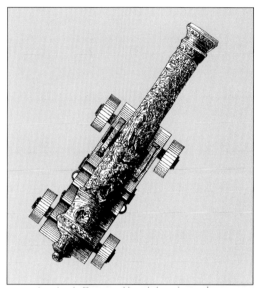
Typical Canon Used by Atondo

soon taken for a sign of his murder by some hostile Indians. Then, an Indian chief unleashed a dud arrow at an officer in the compound, which Atondo took as a sign of hostility. Knowing the fright that had been witnessed when he made a show of force a week or so before, Atondo determined to repeat the show of deadly force with greater effect. An armed band approached the little fort; they were invited to enter the small plaza where they sat down to a meal of pozole. Two small cannons were wheeled up and pointed at the naked Indians who had never experienced their firepower. At the Admiral's command the fuses were lighted and two loud explosions sprayed the dinner party with grape-shot. Three Indians lay dead and the others, scorched and wounded, ran for their lives. To the Spanish mind justice was thus served. No more murders; no more thievery!

But it didn't happen that way. Fear clutched the men on the beach. They waited for a retaliatory attack. They argued about leaving. They prayed for the return of the *Concepción*. The officers voted to wait for relief. The soldiers and settlers petitioned to abandon the hapless venture. A week later Admiral Atondo caved in. And reluctantly Kino and Goñi boarded the jam-packed *San Xavier* that stood out to sea, waiting several days for sight of either the *Concepción* or the long-missing sloop. No one came. So Captain Francisco de Pareda steered into the favorable winds that quickly blew him across the Gulf to San Lucas, today's Agiabampo Bay. Kino's first efforts at evangelizing California were a disconcerting failure. He could draw maps, but he couldn't tell the military where to go!

In the meanwhile, the *Balandra* finally coasted into the Bay of La Paz. It was entirely too peaceful. No ships. No people. Captain Parra's landing party discovered the abandoned fort, a few squash and beans barely alive in the heat, and a well shaded by four palms. Obviously, he had come too late, but where had the soldiers and settlers gone? Parra skirted the coast south to Cabo San Lucas without catching sight of anyone. His crew was restless and uncomfortable; they wanted to return; whether Atondo had survived or not was of little concern because they had now spent six months searching for the colony. Actually, they had missed Atondo by only a day or two, but providentially La Paz was not to be the beginning of Spanish permanence on the peninsula. Parra headed for the mainland and anchored just a few miles south of San Lucas, totally unaware of Atondo's location.

The comi-tragedy of maritime mishaps continued. While the Admiral reconsidered his options to meet his obligations to the King, Kino wrote letters expressing high hopes of an imminent return to the island. There was no doubt in his mind of the excruciating need these peoples were in. And unbeknown to Atondo, the *Concepción* had finally sailed from the mouth of the Yaqui with a full load of cattle, horses, and food. Like Parra on the *Balandra*, Captain Blas de Guzmán managed to miss seeing the other ships, encountered furious contrary winds that blew him back across the Gulf three times, and threw all the live stock overboard to save his ship from sinking! He learned from a fisherman that Atondo was back at San Lucas. What now would be the fate of California?

When Guzmán completed his report to the Admiral, he learned of a new attempt to settle at San Bernabé not far from land's end on the tip of California. At least there would be water and a receptive Indian tribe. But Guzmán quickly changed Atondo's mind because he had seen a huge river well to the north of La Paz. This seemed to be the famous "Río Grande" which others had considered inhabitable. So, after two torrid months of refitting the expedition, the two frigates tacked away from the Sinaloa coast toward a new destiny on the unconquerable island.

THE SECOND ATTEMPT

Weighing anchor on September 29, 1683, the feast of St. Michael Archangel, hopes were running high for a successful new conquest. But the fluky winds again ripped the fleet apart and they did not regroup until October 5 when they sighted the so called Río Grande. While the

1683

Aerial view of the Real de San Bruno looking west

ships rode at anchor the next day, launches from the two vessels carried officers, men, and missionaries ashore at high noon. It was the feast of San Bruno. Erecting a cross in the sandy hill, all knelt and prayed for a special blessing on this renewed effort. Now equipped with horses, the explorers rode inland to a small village and within a short while made contact with many friendly natives. It was a more fortuitous beginning than La Paz.

The events of the following days were routinely similar in picking out a defensible site, assuring themselves of a reliable water supply, and clearing the chosen sites for building. It wasn't too many weeks before the expedition realized that the great river was just a grand arroyo that channeled rain water to the Gulf and then sank into the parched sand. Better places might be found, but it would take time.

In a few short weeks the compound took shape with angled fortifications, a small chapel, quarters for the soldiers, and a three room house for the Jesuits. Atondo ordered the *San Xavier* to return to the mainland for careening and supplies; the *Concepción* returned to the Yaqui river for more livestock and food stuffs. Make no mistake – Atondo was bound and determined to make this expedition succeed; he owed it to the Viceroy and King Carlos II. Fortunately, the *Concepción* needed only a month to make the 300 mile trip; it returned with horses, mules, goats, corn and consoling letters for the colonists and missionaries. While the single relief vessel anchored in the lee of the Isla Coronados, Kino and Atondo began a series of ever widening explorations to map the surrounding terrain. The first formal expedition brought them to the foot of the

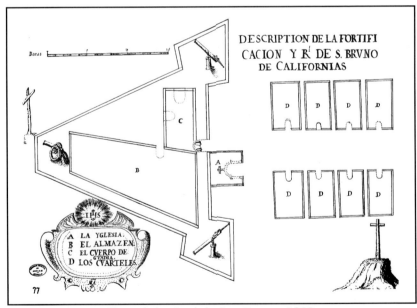

Plan of the Real de San Bruno, 1683

18

Sierra Giganta – so named because it was thought to be the home of giant natives, a myth that has always persisted in Baja California largely due to the enormous cave-paintings scattered all over the peninsula.

December 1, 1683. Well equipped with horses and mules, Kino and Atondo set out with twenty-five soldiers and a contingent of Indian aids. Their goal was to penetrate the Sierra Giganta to the west of San Bruno. It certainly seemed reasonable so well were they prepared. Riding west for three days, they confronted the sheer wall of rock that the mountain presented on its eastern face. There were no obvious trails up the imposing face, so Indian scouts and soldiers scrabbled up using picks and ropes until they reached the heights. There was no possibility of bringing the animals up the cliffs, so the rest of the party dismounted and scaled the rock face as best they could. By nightfall on December 3 the exhausted men looked east to the Gulf and west to the plains that stretched toward the Pacific. They stood on the shoulders of the Giantess and peered into an unknown future. Trudging along the volcanic ash of the trails they reached a shallow lake by nightfall. Appropriately, they named it Laguna de Santa Barbara, as much for the feast day as for the tortures they had experienced in reaching the water hole.

Atondo wasn't wrong in having chosen Kino for his Royal Cartographer, who was now impatient to get over the next band of hills. But Atondo was worn out. He would camp and recoup. Kino could carry on, and he did. With eighteen indefatigable Spaniards and Indians, he set out toward the north. They were carrying supplies for two days only, so the hikers strode out at their best capable speed. Rounding another lake, they encountered a band of armed Indians whom Kino adeptly disarmed by conferring glass beads and red handkerchiefs. The soldiers stood guard and watched in amazement as the blackrobe from the Tyrol used sign language and a few chosen words he had learned in the last months. Kino learned then of a river to the north that flowed down from the crest of the Sierra Giganta to the "Contra Costa," the Pacific. But time, energy, and supplies were lacking to make those explorations. The explorers returned to camp where Atondo was dreaming of the relative comforts of San Bruno. One overnight at the Sepulcher of San Clemente and they were at the edge of the cliffs again. Bumping, scraping, sliding down the precipitous slopes, they arrived at the base camp in time for a siesta and a late afternoon ride toward San Bruno. By noon the next day, the entourage reached San Isidro where Kino celebrated Mass with the luxury of vestments. As the sun set behind the now conquered Sierra Giganta, the second expedition trotted into the Real de San Bruno. All had been a success!

After such an immense expenditure of effort, one would expect Kino to rest well, write his reports, and conjure up something for the holidays. Not so. Feverishly, he wrote up his accounts, drew a detailed map of their adventures, and dashed off letters to friends and fellow Jesuits. He wasted no time because even while the ink of the map was drying, he was again in the saddle with a scout, nine soldiers and five natives. He simply had to find the way to the river that led to the sea. The lean scouting party rode north by northwest as far as a willow-lined stream they named for St. Thomas. The next morning the horsemen moved up the sandy arroyo and discovered that it did indeed penetrate the mountain barrier. Crossing over the summit, they followed an arroyo down more than ten miles. All along the route were signs of good trails and human occupation. By night fall the fires of a near-by village tempted them to stay until the next day. Early in the morning, the party approached the Indian settlement which sent an emissary to inquire about the intruders. Once again, Kino quickly won over the confidence of the Indians, but the problem now became one of making a hasty return because the time allowed for the exploration was running out. With the help of local Indians they found a shorter, if steeper, path down to the Llano de San Pablo, and by ten o'clock on December 24th the jubilant riders were back at San Bruno. What a Christmas present for all concerned because now a full scale expedition could be mounted to the shores of the South Sea! The Goliath of the Sierra Giganta had succumbed to the sling of a determined missionary David.

People always seem to ask, how did Padre Kino spend Christmas? From his diaries we learn that he spent his first Christmas in California, indeed, the first recorded Christmas, European style in California, in joyous celebration. The tiny colony on the mesa of San Bruno set off fire works, sang, feasted, and danced in the church! The merriment continued until midnight when Kino and Goñi solemnly intoned the Mass at Midnight, the first of the three they would each celebrate on Christmas Day. The Admiral had every reason to rejoice at the success of his second *entrada*; his ambitions were vindicated with the affability of the Indians and the achievements at exploration. The symbolism of the birth of Christ was not lost on his perceptions of these new beginnings in the northwest of New Spain. Both God and King were being well served.

A NEW YEAR AND NEW HOPE

Optimism ruled as the new year, 1684, dawned over San Bruno. Soldiers and Indians prepared more fields, quarried rock, shaped adobes – all to strengthen the fortifications and houses spreading along the narrow mesa. Little thought was given to more exploration because the order of the day was the completion of the compound and the growing of essential crops. Already three months had passed since their lone links to the mainland had sailed off, leaving the struggling colony to hope for resupply before spring. But it was not to happen that way. At San Bruno the sun burned away the water, and with the water, the crops; disease swept through the settlement. Unexpected frosts damaged the vegetables, fruits, and melons that had been so meticulously planted in sandy soils once moist with run-off. Kino and Goñi took advantage of the time to learn more of the languages, teach the ever present children, and embellish the chapel with a stone altar decorated with shells from the warm-water shores. Another Lent and another Easter season passed on the peninsula, again without a sail on the horizon. By summer, supplies were dwindling dangerously low; would help never come?

Then, running before a strong summer wind, the *San Xavier* hove into view. It was August 10, 1684, Kino's 39th birthday. What a fine present! But more than the new complement of soldiers, foodstuffs and hardware, the vessel carried news from the mainland, including permission for Kino to take his final vows in the Society! On the feast of the Assumption of Mary, Padre Kino knelt before Father Juan Bautista Copart at the very altar he had built with his own hands. The vows recited, the documents signed, and the "*Suscipe*" said, Kino had completed the long training and probation required of the professed fathers of the Company of Jesus! One can only imagine the emotions that welled up in his heart because the vows symbolized everything he had strived for more than a quarter century. In the midst of deprivation, isolated on a desert island, charged

1684

Ruins of San Bruno where Kino pronounced final vows, 1684

with the responsibility of bringing a new faith to his "abandoned" Indians, and depending on his wits and education, he typified the Jesuit of his times, in fact all times. He was truly like another Francis Xavier.

Atondo immediately ordered the *Almiranta* back to the Río Yaqui to take on the livestock which were awaiting shipment from the Jesuit missions. Although the humid summer air made life uncomfortable, Kino was given a little "R&R" to visit Jesuit companions on the mainland. He would also act as tour guide to Eusebio, a California Indian, who had never before ventured across the Gulf. Landing at the mouth of the Yaqui, the *San Xavier* learned that Atondo's lieutenant, Juan Antonio Anguis, had failed to round up the livestock because he was embroiled in some small insurrections. So Kino's brief vacation turned into a major effort to gather all the livestock and supplies so badly needed in California. The work didn't bother the industrious missioner, and he thrilled at how Eusebio marveled at seeing the opulence of the riverine missions. Within a month the frigate was back at San Bruno off-loading horses, mules, and pack animals. At last California seemed to have a reliable supply system. Over the next two months the ship made three more successful crossings and brought some forty-two horses, twenty-two mules, and a host of sheep. It began to look promising for a new expedition, but the

San Xavier was falling apart from hard use; it was ordered to Matanchel for refitting – if it could survive the voyage, and luckily it made port two days before Christmas.

THE GREAT EXPEDITION

No sooner had the frigate stood off to sea than Kino and Atondo mounted their horses for the ride to San Isidro which was the staging ground for the expedition to cross the "island." Ample water and forage made it far more ideal than drought stricken San Bruno. Kino was confident of Indian loyalty and assured Atondo of the safety in taking the majority of the soldiers along on the difficult trip. Perhaps the exploratory party was more grandiose than the terrain should merit, but the organizers felt they would find far greener pastures along the "river to

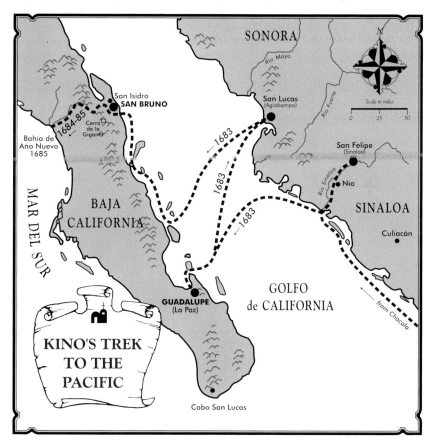

the west." Forty-three persons, including Kino, Atondo, soldiers, muleteers, and baggage handlers, and ninety-one mounts clopped out of San Isidro the morning of December 15; an adventure was in the making.

The route was the same. North to the Arroyo of Santo Tomás. What had taken Kino a day the year before now took three days because trees had to be cut, rocks removed, and a basic trail prepared before the cavalcade could thread its way toward the imposing mountain barrier. Finally, December 19, the big push was on. Horses, mules, and pack animals churned up the steep slopes in clouds of dust. It took every bit of animal energy that man and beast could muster to surmount the rugged trail; by nightfall the exhausted train reached the summit in high hopes of seeing sparkling streams. The only sparkle was the glint of sun on stones in the Arroyo de Comondú. For three difficult days they worked their way down to the conjunction with the Río La Purísima. Thanks be to God, there was water enough in the rocky stream to drive a mill wheel if any grain were around to be processed. The flowing waters had to lead eventually to the sea, so the weary men and animals followed its rugged meanderings southward through boulder strewn canyons. Again, it was Christmastide. But this time there was no feasting or dancing. Horses

A View of the Purísima Canyon to Northwest

slipped on the rocks; mules fell into hidden pools, lush undergrowth had to be hacked away to permit passage. They had arrived on Noche Buena (Christmas Eve), but it had turned into a nightmare for survival. Camping at San Estevan (a fitting dedication since it was December 26 the feast of the proto-martyr who had been stoned to death for loyalty to his faith), men and horses spent a whole day resting and healing their sore selves. This was certainly no paradise, but the word from Indian guides told them the South Sea was not far off. Continuing down the Purísima drainage, they stopped at

Sombrero Peak at Purísima

Los Innocentes, naming yet another place by the liturgical patron of the day. Kino and some stalwart soldiers climbed a hat-shaped peak to survey the surroundings; his telescope seemed to see the ocean, but ever the skeptical scientist, Kino only hoped, not hollered.

Two weeks of tremendous effort had been expended, and the explorers were nearly in sight of their goal. Since the animals were over-taxed and in need of serious recuperation, Atondo and Kino chose eighteen mounted men, three Indians, and two pack animals to press on to the coast. The next day they covered sixteen miles, stopping at Santo Tomás. On the 30th the anxious riders reached the estuary, known today as San Gregorio, and trotted westward with anticipation until their horses slowed in the sands.

Not far below the surf crashed along the shore that stretched ever northward. What a sight! What an accomplishment! It was the first time ever that Europeans had crossed the great island by land. And it was a feat that few Indians themselves had done because the abrasive volcanic ash that covers the ground made walking long distances nearly impos-

Pacific shore near Bahía Año Nuevo

sible. The explorers broke tradition by naming the long estuary they had seen, Bahía Año Nuevo. Unfortunately, that historic name has given way to San Gregorio so few people are reminded of the momentous accomplishments of Kino's first crossing. Wouldn't it be wonderful if the maps and coastal charts would remind us of that bright day in January, 1685, when these dauntless explorers, like Balboa, crossed an arm between the seas to gaze on the pounding Pacific?

1685

RETURN AND RETREAT

More sand, more rocks, more desolate country was all the expedition saw in its arduous return over the spine of the Giantess. San Bruno was a pleasant sight even if its stores were diminishing and disease was threatening soldier and settler alike. Atondo now realized that it had become urgent to find more promising lands with a reliable, sweet water supply. Leaving Kino behind to devise maps of the explorations, he set out with Padre Goñi to probe the canyons farther south for a route to Magdalena Bay. For three weeks the anxious scouting party assailed the rocky slopes only to be rebuffed time and again. Returning by the narrow coastal trail, they arrived at beleaguered San Bruno March 6. They had found no trails west, no pasturage, no water source – only scattered

Indian rancherías with small brush huts. They found San Bruno even more destitute. The food supplies were nearly gone; the water, brackish; the settlers, sullen. It seemed as though California was slipping from Atondo's grasp when a slender young lad stumbled into camp guided by friendly Indians from the south. He clutched messages from the captain of the *Balandra* now anchored nearby in San Dionisio Bay. Replenished with essential supplies from the sloop, San Bruno took a new lease on life, and in less than three more weeks, the *Concepción* dropped anchor off shore from the lone Spanish *real*. Indians and crewmen waded to the beach with bales of desperately needed supplies. But what was needed most of all – fresh fruits and vegetables – was not aboard in sufficient quantity. The scurvy that was laying the settlement low continued to surge ahead. By April 9 Atondo's sense of reality was sternly shaken because only fifteen men answered muster; two score and four others were too sick or dying. With the advice and consent of the officers, he issued orders to prepare to abandon San Bruno. Kino was crushed because he saw no purpose in leaving the gentle, trusting Indians behind. The very purpose of the expedition had been to evangelize the "island." But now, because no pearls and no rich lands were found, the Spaniards were leaving!

The mission Rector's objections were over-ruled and thin lines of burden-bearing men threaded their way to the long boats as the treasures of San Bruno were packed up for the voyage to the mainland. The best horses were slung aboard, the rest, were left to their fate with the starving Indians. May 8 was not a happy day for California. The months of intense labor, the months of anxious waiting – for rain, for sight of a sail, for news of a discovery – they were all over. Now they only waited for a favorable breeze to bring the sick and disillusioned quickly across the gulf. Two days later, the sick were hurried off to the Jesuit mission of Torím on the Río Yaqui. And Kino fought off grief with prayers of resignation to God's will. What a strange language, that of the Divine.

Actually, Padre Kino had eked a concession out of Atondo. He was to reconnoiter the coast north of San Bruno perhaps to discover better lands in cooler latitudes. A nice theory, but this was after all a land-locked gulf, not an island, as Kino had yet to prove. No matter how far north they might sail on the Sea of Cortez, it would be forever hot, dry, and desolate. But Captain Guzmán of the *Concepción* was determined to discharge his responsibility. The frigate sailed west from the Río Yaqui straight to the passages east of the Tres Virgenes, the sometimes active volcanoes mid-way up the gulf. Once again the fickle winds of summer blasted the ship to and fro until he had to seek refuge in a cratered bay at the mouth of the Sonora River. As fate would have it, this very place is known today as Kino Bay, but not to Guzmán. For forty-five days the ship dragged anchor in the shelter of small hills while Guzmán sought some kind of northerly passage. He found none that he felt reliable. And Kino, to his credit, went ashore to befriend the Seris who lived along the estuary. It was a labor of sheer love in the searing heat of July. And by the time Guzmán returned, in defeat, Kino's continuing presence was fervently desired by the skillful natives. Little did Kino know that the river banks where he was teaching the rudiments of Christianity were shaped by a river that flowed down from the land of his future destiny, the Pimería Alta. But the cosmographer/missionary could not stay. Stage by stage Providence was blocking wrong directions and beckoning better ones.

The winds shifted long enough for the *Concepción* to escape its forced anchorage at Kino Bay. Putting in again at the Río Yaqui, the flagship took on the now recuperated soldiers and settlers. Guzmán hoisted sail and set a course through stormy seas for San Bruno, not to stock the abandoned *real*, but to leave off some Indian children who had gone

Kino Bay, Sonora

with Kino to see the mainland. San Bruno looked as though God was rebuking Atondo because recent rains had ended the long drought; the countryside was lush and green. Nevertheless, the orders were to return to Matanchel. Then, three days out of San Bruno, the *Concepción* spied the sloop at anchor off the Island of Carmen. Atondo was still trying to fill the nearly empty treasure chest with measly pearls to offer the viceroy as compensation for the immense expenditures of a failed expedition. Parting company with the pearl fishers, Guzmán steered the frigate to Matanchel, dropping anchor September 17. Kino lost no time ascending the steep trails to Guada-

Santispac, BCS

lajara to report to Bishop Garabito; he could register a plea with him for an immediate return to California. After all the *San Xavier* was careened and ready; the crew was available; and the drought was definitively ended.

PIRATES INTERVENE

Throughout the summer since the abandonment of San Bruno communiqués were racing between Mexico City, Guadalajara and the coastal cities. Viceroy Paredes reiterated his strong support of the California venture despite the set-backs and expense. The object of the expedition from the beginning had been the conversion of the native populace, and nothing was going to prevent that from being accomplished. King Carlos would pay for all. Kino learned of the viceroy's decision with characteristic enthusiasm. Even though the missionaries had baptized only eleven infants in all their time in California, the natives were peaceful, docile, and eventually would embrace the faith. Crossing paths in Compostela, Kino and Atondo spoke assuringly of an immediate return. Meanwhile the Admiral was off to see the viceroy, and Kino headed down to Matanchel to meet Padre Copart where they would prepare for an imminent departure. The *San Xavier* was refitted and ready to sail.

Then, Admiral Atondo clattered into town with news that the viceroy had ordered the "Armada of the Californias" to find and escort the Manila galleon to Acapulco. Four or five Dutch pirates were lurking in the harbor of La Navidad to waylay the unsuspecting treasure ship. With luck the three California ships encountered the lumbering galleon the second day, escorting it back to Chacala. With Kino aboard the China ship, the frigates guided the galleon well clear of La Navidad and lead it safely to heavily fortified Acapulco. This short cruise was as close as Kino would ever get to his dreams of sailing off to the land of Francis Xavier. Instead the padre mounted a mule and braved the precipitous trail to Mexico City where he regaled fellow Jesuits with tales of the California conquest. Now that Atondo's tiny armada had foiled the plans of Spillbergen, there would be a certain claim on the riches that had been protected. Viceroy Paredes, indeed, looked most favorably on the continuance of the California project despite the meager return of pearls and precious metals; after all, the primary object was the conversion of the peoples of the island.

1686

Diplomacy and Disappointment

Two months passed in the capital. A full dress conference on the island expedition confirmed the Crown's commitment, and the arrival of a silver train from Zacatecas insured that the administration could pay for the costs of California, estimated at 30,000 pesos. Although there had been repeated reversals that had fed Atondo's critics, his misadventure was becoming high drama. The *San Xavier* and the sloop were again assigned to launch a new attempt across the gulf. Everything was building toward a much better future – until the flota of '86 arrived carrying decrees from the King that demolished all at the stroke of a pen. Years before, a French treasure ship was sunk in the Bay of Cádiz, and the King of France wanted immediate recompense, a mere 500,000 pesos. All available money was to be returned to Spain forthwith! And if that was not enough of a blow to California, the viceroy was also ordered to render aid to Nueva Vizcaya immediately in order to stave off a rumored rebellion, even if it meant suspending the vaunted return to California. Padre Kino was stunned. His Belgian companion, Padre Copart came mentally unglued and spent the rest of his years struggling with the trauma; what the austerity of California had failed to accomplish was swiftly done by a distant bureaucracy.

What now? Kino was mission rector without a mission. He had learned a language unspoken on the mainland. He was a mathematician without figures, a cartographer without unexplored lands, a priest without a people. Would anything ever go right for the altruistic Tyrolese who had abandoned his fatherland for a New World that appeared always to be rejecting him as a prodigal son on the wrong side of the sea?

Whoever has dealt with people on either slope of the Alps will usually confirm that some of the most diplomatic persons on earth hail from these mountain fastnesses. When the Council of Trent was convened to debate the theology of a Protestant Europe, strong overtones of Alpine diplomacy permeated the gathering. And somehow those political skills had penetrated the person of Padre Kino. He had done admirably well with the native populace of California, and now with the definitive abandonment of the island his whole future was compromised. May in Mexico City was crammed with the memories of a whole year which had its high points, not the least of which was the torrid July spent on the estuary of the Sonora River while Guzmán searched for a northern passage. Kino approached the Count and Countess Paredes with a request – could he be permitted to return to the Seri-Guaymas coast? Those people were in such dire need and they were, after all, as close to California as he could get without disobeying the King's commands.

Skillfully, Kino plied his vaunted diplomacy on the powers of New Spain. And surprisingly, all concurred in his proposal. He would be allowed to establish three missions on the coast with all the attendant subsidies. Waiting until November, Kino left the capital for Guadalajara where he petitioned the Audiencia for a ruling to free any converts from the imposition of the *repartamiento*, the practice of involuntary servitude, for a period of five years. The President and Council agreed completely, but they preferred to enforce a recent cédula of the Crown that exempted converts for twenty years! Elated with the ruling, he realized that he had in hand a veritable emancipation proclamation for colonial New Spain. He rode out before nightfall and made his way west and north; the trails were familiar, but the future, unpredictable. At the moment he had sufficient funds for two missions and the promise of the assignment of Father Adam Gilg as his companion – or least that was the thinking of Father Provincial Bernabé de Soto, who had taken over from Luis del Canto, Kino's provincial superior during the California years.

By now one would think that Kino would be wary of any new assignment. Already he had witnessed how troubles on a frontier could disrupt the most meticulous plans made in a distant capital. As Kino rode confidently toward the bay that would later bear his name, events in the Province of Sonora were shaping a quite different destination. The northern frontier had been devastated by the revolt of the Pueblos in 1680. Spanish colonists had been driven out of New Mexico and native alliances were conjoined to prevent their return. Although New Mexico was revered by the Spanish settlers for its land and climate, it had never offered any mineral riches. Chihuahua and Sonora, on the other hand, encompassed vast resources that had to be protected at all costs. Against this backdrop of rebellion and alliance word had been circulating that the Pimas Altas were on the verge of aligning themselves with the Pueblos to cut off any Spanish advance into the northwest. Miners, settlers, and missionaries met in Sonora to appeal for a special missionary to be sent to the Pimería Alta in order to offset any Piman involvement that might seal the frontier. Unsuspecting, Kino would arrive at Oposura to report to Padre Manuel González, the visitor of the northwest missions. On González's desk lay a request from the Alcalde Mayor of Sonora, Antonio Barba de Figuera, that the next missionary to come to the north ought to be immediately assigned to the Pimería Alta. Kino was next. It would be months before he saw Kino Bay and the Seri Indians again because he was now headed for the "Rim of Christendom." At last, his convoluted destiny was unfolding. The future was beckoning him to sprawling deserts and stubby mountains, to blue skies and stark saguaros, to frustration and fame.

THE RIM OF CHRISTENDOM

Travel along the Sinaloa coast was no novelty for the "Padre on Horseback." The months spent in outfitting the California expedition had acquainted him with missions and Spanish towns scattered over the series of deltas below the escarpment of the Sierra Madre Occidental. This time, however, Kino had to consult with the regional superior, Padre Manuel González at Oposura in central Sonora. His most convenient route took him north of the old stronghold of El Fuerte where Francisco Ibarra, the 16th century explorer, built his headquarters. The Camino Real twisted through Los Frailes, the recently discovered mines which later became Alamos, the "mint city" of the northwest. Spending a few days there, Kino became acquainted with Domingo Terán de los Ríos, the alcalde who in just a few years would become the first governor of Texas and would cross Kino's path in one of the most significant episodes in Kino's missionary career. He rested and reflected a short while at the Jesuit mission of Conicari where he displayed a genuine enthusiasm for the silver discoveries because he suspected they would mean even more apostolic aid from the Crown. Impressed but not distracted by the promise of riches, he worked his way through the cactus canyons and tortured trails to Oposura on the Río Moctezuma. He was so deep into the mountains now any view of distant California dwelled only in his imagination.

In the sharp cold of March he found Father Visitor González preparing to celebrate the feast of the canonization of Sts. Ignatius and Francis Xavier. He would present his papers for the founding of the Seri missions, but Padre González, who as visitador was effectively the vice-provincial, overruled those plans because of the urgency of the situation in the Pimería Alta. Father Aguilar, the minister at Cucurpe, had urged an assignment to the new mission territory at Cosari, a Piman village slightly north of Cucurpe, the placid Opata town on the San Miguel. Once again California slipped from Kino's grasp – only this time it would be permanent, or almost so! No time was to be lost in responding to the Pimas' request for a missionary priest, particularly now that Kino was carrying legal relief from forced labor in the mines, a practice that was threatening the stability of the frontier. Nor did they delay. The two Blackrobes crossed the colorful outcroppings of the mountains into the

1687

Sonora Valley, the scene of so much significant Spanish history in the north – this was the path of Fray Marcos de Niza, Francisco Vásquez de Coronado, and Francisco Ibarra. It was the way to the Tierra Incognita Adentro, the unknown interior. If California was to be left uncharted, Kino at least had a whole new land to explore and map.

Cucurpe, "where the doves sing," was Father José Aguilar's last outpost. Beyond lay the Pimería Alta. Strangely, this perimeter had not been penetrated since a two man Jesuit expedition in the late 1640s. After the death of Governor Pedro de Perea (1645), the Jesuits decided to send Fathers Francisco Paris and Pedro Bueno among the Hymeris, the "raven people" – actually the old name for the Pimas Altas. But for political reasons the expedition was suspended. Then, as Providence would have it, the full retinue of horses, mules, and livestock that had been rounded up for the trip, "unattended," completed a miraculous circuit of the land of the Hymeris, visiting all their villages and returning without a scratch! Being obedient, of course, the two Jesuits patiently awaited the animals return! *(Obedezco pero no cumplo* –I obey, but I don't comply). And now forty years later it was Kino's turn.

Finishing the Novena of Grace, a nine-day devotion honoring the canonization of St. Ignatius and St. Francis Xavier, on their arrival at

---

Prayer of the Novena of Grace

Oh most lovable and loving St. Francis Xavier, in union with you, I reverently adore the Divine Majesty. While giving joyful thanks to God for the singular gifts of grace bestowed upon you during life and your gifts of glory after death, I ask you with deepest devotion to obtain for me the greatest of all blessings: the grace of living a decent life and dying a holy death. Moreover, I beg you to obtain for me *(state the favor you ask)*. If what I ask of you so earnestly does not tend to the glory of God and the great good of my soul, please intercede, I pray that I may receive what is best for both. AMEN. *(Here recite the Our Father, Hail Mary, and Glory Be.)*

Pray for us, St. Francis Xavier, that we may be made worthy of the promises of Christ.

Let us pray. Almighty God you were pleased to bring into the Church the nations of the Indies through the preaching and miracles of St. Francis Xavier, mercifully grant that we who venerate his glorious merits may also follow the example of his virtues. Through Christ Our Lord. AMEN.

Cucurpe, the two experienced missionaries and Padre Kino cantered out of town in the brisk morning air of March 13, 1687. Destination, history.

By mid-day they had negotiated the twelve winding miles up the Río San Miguel to Cosari, a humble native village on a bluff overlooking a gentle valley south of the imposing peak of the Sierra Azul. The Pimas were ecstatic to know that the request of decades was being fulfilled that very day. Kino carefully unwrapped a rolled oil painting, a gift of the renowned Mexican artist Juan Correa. It was

Our Lady of Sorrows

a stunning portrait of Our Lady of Sorrows, under whose patronage Kino had promised to place the first of his new missions. Just as he had promised the Duchess of Aveiro to name the first mission in California after Our Lady of Guadalupe, so now he named Cosari in the Pimería, Nuestra Señora de los Dolores. Gently, he placed the painting on the crude altar that had been built in anticipation of his coming. How sad that that artistic treasure has been lost, due to centuries of abuse and neglect.

Typical of the enthusiastic Kino, the very next day he saddled up and rode across the intervening mountain to the village of Caburica, nestled in a shallow valley a few miles south of the heartland of the Hymeris, today known as Imuris. Still remembering the intense days of the Novena of Grace that were celebrated on horseback in arriving at his first mission post, Kino dedicated his second mission here at Caburica in honor of the founder of the Jesuit Order, Ignatius Loyola; actually it was at Padre González's express order. On March 15 they were again on the trail upstream to Imuris which was given to the patronage of San José, slightly in anticipation of his feast, but more likely in honor of Padre Aguilar who had prepared the way for the coming of a new missionary. All that was left now was to complete the circuit and return to Dolores by way of the

Río Cocóspera. As always, it was stunning country in the burst of spring. The streams were gushing, the cottonwoods beginning to show their light green leaves, and the ocotillo, their bright red flowers. It was spring in Sonora and spring for the new conversions. All that remained now was the serene ride through red rock canyons and over oak covered slopes on the return to Dolores. Kino had staked out his new mission land, and he was unquestionably thrilled. So many peaks to climb, so many canyons and caves to explore. And so very many docile Indians to befriend, to educate, and convert, God willing. Kino was atop the rim of Christendom and he was mapping out a future that would make history.

The Pimería Alta — A New Mission Field

The Jesuit practice in mission expansion was a carefully devised program. New missions were established only among the more permanent native settlements. The initial foundation was kept reasonably close to already functioning missions for physical and moral support. Padre Eusebio followed that practice by locating his home base, Nuestra Señora de los Dolores, at Cosari, only slightly higher up the shallow mountain valley from Cucurpe. His new site would be close, but quite independent. And Cosari was an ideal spot because his church and compound

Valley of the San Miguel north of Dolores

dominated two valleys separated by a narrow defile that closed down on the clear waters of the Río San Miguel..

The enthusiasm of Padre Kino became the catalyst for a new desert economy! The Pimans had farmed their lands for many generations, but never did they achieve so much as under their new missionary. Drowsy deltas sprang into productive gardens. River lands were cleared for wheat, corn and squash; slopes were readied for grapes and imported European fruit trees. Each village in the new mission rectorate erected an adobe chapel and started the long-term work on the churches which would be the pride of their pueblos. And the names that Kino bestowed on the new towns have become bywords in Southwestern history – San Ignacio, Magdalena, San Xavier del Bac, Cocóspera, Caborca, Tumacácori, and Tucson. Some names Christian, some names Indian, but all recorded in time through the industry of their founder and provider.

The hard years were the early years. Kino's presence was not appreciated by the miners along the Bacanuche and the San Miguel, nor did the hechiceros (medicine men) take kindly to the threat to their tribal power and superstitious practices. But a program of patience with the natives and forthrightness with the Spaniards smashed opposition to change and Christianization. The little chain of missions on Padre Kino's seventy-five mile circuit was mushrooming. Padre González remarked that he had never seen such growth in such a short time.

Obviously, the expanding missions didn't happen out of thin air. Kino appealed to neighboring Jesuit missions for whatever aid they could furnish. In quick response Padre Antonio Rojas, who had taken over the administration of Ures and the missions on the lower San Miguel, supplied Kino with livestock and a little silver. More importantly, two Indian converts joined Kino at Dolores where Francisco Cantor assisted in training the community in new techniques of farming and animal husbandry. And his blind brother brought many to the light of the Gospel with his keen abilities in language and the catechism. Typical of Padre Kino, he lost no time in organizing his neophytes and drawing them willingly into a vibrant community. They must have been impressed because just two weeks after Kino's arrival, they accompanied him to the festivities of Holy Week at Tuape only a few miles downstream from Cucurpe. To anyone who travels the sandy valleys of central Sonora,

Holy Week is still celebrated with fervent pagentry. One can imagine how Tuape looked in March, 1687, when Kino rode into town with more than a hundred Pimans from his new mission to join in with the scores of Spaniards and Opatas from the Río Sonora and others from farther south. The dramatization of the events of Holy Week made the mysteries of Christianity immediate and impactful. Good and evil were visually portrayed in relation to the suffering and death of Jesus and the sorrowing of Mary. Kino must have reflected on the stark contrast of these celebrations with those he had performed at La Paz and San Bruno.

1687

Spring was a time for building. In a matter of a few weeks an adobe chapel rose up on the mesa top overlooking the Cosari valley to the north; a humble house for the priest was tucked into the edge of the bluff below the chapel. There, an acequia directed fresh river water alongside the house and into an ample orchard studded with a variety of fruit trees and vines. Some day Dolores would reap the joys of Kino's industry. Almost instinctively, Kino sensed that Dolores would be his home for many years to come, unless of course, he found a way to return to California. Hardly had the first church been completed than bells arrived from Mexico City; they were hung in a sturdy *espadaña* and rang out the *Angelus* each day and the *De Profundis* at night. Every aspect of life was being touched by Kino's enthusiasm and hard work. And probably more significant than anything else in those first months at Dolores was the conversion of Chief Coxi and his family. Already his two sons had received baptism, and Coxi quickly followed suite. This was a whole new approach that Coxi realized was of benefit to himself and his people. The chief was not merely a village headman; his jurisdiction extended over the whole of the Pimería, even to the shores of the Gulf. Like a mini-Constantine, Coxi's conversion sent a powerful signal throughout the Pima nation that the acceptance of Christianity at the hands of a man like Padre Eusebio was something to be seriously considered.

The first year at Dolores was spent in building a powerful mission base from which to reach out to the scattered Piman settlements to the west and north. Churches and modest living quarters were erected at San Ignacio and Imuris. The Indian builders, assisted by a handful of soldiers, shaped the adobes and raised the walls of missions-to-be. Only at near-by Remedios did Kino encounter troubling resistance. One sus-

1688

pects that there were factions living here who resented the presence and power of Chief Coxi, but at any rate the shamans of the village spread defamatory tales about the newly arrived missionary. They spurned the guarantees of the cédula granting freedom from forced labor for twenty years. Grim reports – rooted in jealousy – began to circulate about the "ambitious Padre Kino" and the "quarrelsome Indians in his charge." Both civil and religious superiors across the multiple mountain barriers became wary of this new man on their frontier. Although such reports were endemic to Spanish colonial life, they had to be investigated.

A GRIM FACED INSPECTOR ARRIVES

After only a year and a half of intense work in building, raising cattle, harvesting crops, planting trees and vines, Father Visitor González arrived on a circuit of inspection. He confessed that in all his years of missionary experience, he had never witnessed such stupendous growth and expansion in so short a time. Since Fathers Marcos Kappus and Adam Gilg, who were originally supposed to assist Kino, had been assigned to other missions to the south, Kino appealed to González to recruit other new missionaries to help him in the Pimería. The long, labor-intensive days were building up a missionary base nearly unequaled elsewhere in the desert, and the flourishing new missions were ready to be turned over to willing new recruits. González agreed, and in a few months four Jesuits accepted missions at San Ignacio, Tubutama, Sáric, and Cocóspera. Their presence would now let Kino the explorer be free to roam the frontier.

Juan María Salvatierra, S.J.

1689

But at the same time, discontent with Padre Kino's growing influence fanned the flames of rumor about there being no need for so many Jesuit missionaries among so few natives. Was that really true since the baptisms were being recorded in the high hundreds? Or was it because the Pimas had been such an easy target for slaving parties from the mining reales in the east? Jesuit presence in the opinion of many colonials was not an ideal condition. More complaints were circulated about the "Padre Cariblanco," a pejorative name imported from the Caribbean. They didn't like Kino's stern demands for justice; they didn't like his Germanic accent; they didn't appreciate his popularity with the Indians. They just plain didn't like him being around. So even more complaints boiled out of San Juan Bautista and the surrounding mining camps. Something would have to be done if they were to maintain control over their previously unprotected labor pool. Conversion of the native populace threatened their customary, easy exploitation. What Spaniard wanted to risk his life picking out silver ore from narrow ledges in deep, damp mines? That was work for Indians.

Padre González's inspection did not deliver results that pleased Kino's critics, so they vigorously complained to the provincial in Mexico City. In response, the provincial dispatched Padre Juan María Salvatierra, the future giant of Lower California, from his mountain mission in Chínipas to visit the missions of Sonora just before Christmas, 1690. Exercising the powers of a Jesuit Visitor General, his primary task was to review the situation on the "rim" and shut down Kino's missions if conditions even approached the rumors rampant in the interior. The Mexican provincial, himself an experienced missionary, knew that hawk-nosed Salvatierra would be strong enough to quiet Kino down – after all they were both Italians by birth. It looked like a case of Providence bringing Kino to the brink of disaster all over again.

1690

Lesser men would have crumbled under the hardships, the criticism, and the mere threat of another total failure by abandoning the new mission field. But Kino, true to form, met the Padre Visitador with real warmth and genuine enthusiasm. Together Kino and Salvatierra rode the hundreds of leagues linking the mission visitas. The land was flush with crops; villagers greeted the Blackrobes by erecting crosses and flowered arches. Indians trudged in from distant pueblos to beg Baptism for themselves and their families. Every hour of travel saw a panorama of plenty, and every hour of rest received the Indians' pleas for the Faith and a missionary.

League by league the long face of Salvatierra shortened; the anticipated harshness of his task was mellowed by what he saw. He had expected to find a frontier in disarray and a populace that dissimulated rebellion. His naturally gaunt features were deceptive because he could hardly fail to recognize the accomplishments of his countryman. Animated conversations on horseback suggested whole new worlds of apostolic endeavor. Finally a smile broke beneath his hawked features as he contemplated the prospects of Christianizing this happy land. Salvatierra heard as much as he saw, because Kino talked of the island of California and the imminent conversion of her peoples. He even suggested the construction of a boat to ply across the Gulf. Why not? The riches of Sonora could supply the wants of California!

By the time Salvatierra was ready to continue south through the extensive Jesuit missions along the Yaqui and Mayo rivers, he had learned to share the abiding vision of Padre Eusebio. The profound conviction imparted by the Apostle to the Pimas not only staved off the foreclosure of the Sonora mission effort, but it also decided Salvatierra on courageously regaining the Californias. A whole new dimension had dawned for the Pimería. Padre Kino, remembering the extreme need of the peninsular people, pressed efforts to make his missions even more productive. Success in Sonora meant life for the Church in California. No one knew better than Kino and Salvatierra that without cooperation and mutual sacrifice any missionary venture is untenable and doomed to sterility.

One of the touching episodes of Salvatierra's inspection happened at Tumacácori, under the "Belted Mountain." Scores of Pimas from the north converged there carrying crosses and flowered arches in a convincing appeal for more Blackrobes to reside in their villages. Salvatierra then realized that Kino had not exaggerated about the genuineness of the Piman people. To close down these missions and deny such docile and industrious natives the opportunity to enjoy the benefits of the Spanish empire would be a grave injustice. Indeed, the destiny of California, an unknown and undeveloped wonderland, was sealed beneath the "Belted Mountain" when Salvatierra accepted Kino's proposition that the Pimería could nurture the island to the west.

1691

Kino would have to await the decision of the Provincial once Salvatierra reached Mexico City. But it would probably be *pro forma* because the Visitor General left so completely impressed that he revealed his own decision, namely, that not only would he refuse to reassign the four priests now helping Kino, but that he would ask for four more, and with some luck he would be one of them! These were wishes more than decisions because on his return to Mexico, the Milanese missionary was named rector of the novitiate at Tepotzotlán where he piously erected a special shrine to his patroness, Our Lady of Loreto. Kino's companions were not reassigned for several months, but they did eventually receive other posts in the north. Kino would have to train another squad for his spiritual conquest of the Pimería.

CONSOLIDATING A FRONTIER

Instead of bridling Kino's enthusiasm for the Pimería, Salvatierra's visit had stirred up his innate desires of exploration and expansion. Throughout the spring and fall Kino dedicated himself to strengthening his base at Dolores and to assist fellow missionaries at San Ignacio, Tubutama, and Cocóspera. These were critical months because he realized that unless the harvest was plentiful there would be little to entice the Pimas of the north and west to welcome new mission establishments. Spending long hours in teaching, catechizing, planting and irrigating, Kino labored together with his skilled Indian workers. They knew well how to produce crops from the arid land, but they had never experienced the sense of economic and social purpose that seemed to consume the Blackrobe from the Tyrol. All of 1691 passed quietly into history with no significant events to distract the missionary from his work.

Then, Kino's critics found cause to revile the industrious Pimas. In early February, 1692, two droves of mares were rustled from the mission farm of Cuchuta by an alliance of Jocomes, Sumas, and Sobaipuris. Padre Antonio Heredia, the Jesuit in charge, clamored for help from the Compañía Volante at Janos. For many Spaniards on the northern frontier of Sonora this bold intrusion was certain proof that the Sobaipuri Pimas were as hostile as any Apaches, and the event seemed to put the lie to Kino's claims about their peacefulness. Captain Ramírez de Salazár, the elderly Indian fighter, tracked the stolen herd far down the present Río San Pedro. At Baicatcán he cajoled the Piman leaders to give up the herd and make peace. They complied, but still skeptical, he returned south with the Indian leaders to meet Padre Kino. The Blackrobe's reputation

1692

for peace-making had spread throughout the region. Ramírez spent a few days recuperating his retinue of men and horses while the Indians appealed to Kino for inclusion in the program of evangelization. It was a deciding moment for Kino because he realized the critical importance of incorporating the Sobaipuris of the northeast lest they spoil the reputation of docility and peace that their tribal relatives enjoyed in the west. And it was a deciding moment for Sonora as well because Captain Ramírez proposed a definitive plan for protecting the northern frontier with an expanded flying company to be based at Corodeguachi, the future Fronteras.

While Captain Ramírez rode off to Mexico City to present the regional consensus on defense, Padre Kino seized the opportunity to draw the eastern Sobaipuris into his growing domain of converts. Firm guarantees of peace would furnish secure foundations for the Faith because peace and justice were fundamental to Kino's plan for conversion. As harvest time approached, a major expedition was prepared to penetrate the northern and eastern limits of the Pimería. More than a year had elapsed since Kino had promised to visit the village of Bac in response to the devout display of crosses and woven arches. In late August he set out with Indian officials, servants, and fifty pack animals. The trail led north through Remedios, Cocóspera, Tumacácori, to Bac where he met some 800 natives. Kino was so impressed with the people and the environs, he dedicated this largest of Piman villages to St. Francis Xavier, his life-long patron. What an event for the explorer-missionary. He laid out an elaborate map of the world and explained to the huddled Indians how far he had traveled to preach the Gospel. Not only did he point out the location of Dolores which was close enough for them to comprehend, but he pointed out Mexico, the oceans, Europe, and the Holy Land. Maybe Kino was a missionary, but he never ceased being the professor! Into his lecture on geography he wove the tale of St. James and the conversion of Spain which resisted his efforts for fourteen years. But now the Spaniards were committed to the conversion of the world, thus explaining their presence in the land of the Pimas Altas. Without question, Kino's was a global vision even in these remote deserts.

From San Xavier del Bac the expedition made its way east to the Río San Pedro where the Indian leaders he had met months before at

Dolores awaited him in their extensive villages. As the cavalcade looped its way up river to Quiburi, the home of Chief Coro, and then westward along the tributary of the Babacomari, the whole Pimería was being cinched into a new alliance of peace and mutual protection against the marauders from the hills and valleys of the Gila River. Five years of constant travel, negotiations, and service to the native peoples were beginning to pay off for everyone's benefit. It was now time to concentrate on finishing the new church at Dolores.

Buildings and Boats

The winter of 1692 found Padre Kino busily directing his team of carpenters and laborers in the final touches of the domed church in the village of Cosari which overlooked a wide valley of the Río San Miguel. Beyond was the backdrop of the Sierra Azul which defines the topography of the region because all drainages to the north, south, and west spin from its flanks. So when Kino issued invitations to the dedication of the new church, Indians from all over the Pimería easily found their way to his headquarters. Easter was over and the celebrations were set for Saturday, April 26, 1693. The Jesuits converged on Cosari. And the day had all the earmarks of a typical fiesta: the Mass was sung by Padre Juan Muñoz de Burgos; Padre George Hostinski preached; the Pimas danced and sang

1692

1693

Puerto Lobos on the Seri-Tepoca Gulf Coast

in full regalia; young and old feasted on meats, corn, beans, and fresh tortillas. It was spring and the Pimería had genuinely come to life.

Although the happenings on the San Pedro had drawn Kino northward in '92, he never lost sight of his goal, shared with Salvatierra, of returning to the "abandoned" peoples of California. Other Jesuits had been sent to assist him in staffing the growing number of missions. His own church was finally finished and now there would be time to spend in helping the other missionaries in the district. Many assignments had been changed because of the recent revolt in the Tarahumara when two Jesuits were martyred; the ripple effect reached as far as the Pimería. In December, 1693, Kino greeted Padre Agustín de Campos, a native of Huesca (Spain), and brought him along on a circuit of Piman country soon to be opened to missionization. Their pre-Christmas trip took them far west to the land of Chief Soba whose subjects had harbored no little animosity for the Pimas of the foothills.

Just as Kino had done with Coro in the northeast, so too he befriended Soba, forging a lasting peace among the tribes to the far west. Kino, Campos, and Captain Sebastián Romero worked their way up to the highest peak they could see from Caborca where they had met with Chief Soba. Naming the small mountain *"El Nazareno,"* they realized they were still a substantial distance from the glistening shores of the Gulf. That day at the beach would have to wait. Returning to Caborca, the community was christened Nuestra Señora de La Concepción at the request of Father Antonio Leal, the Visitor. It would have to await its first missionary in the spring – also at the order of Father Leal. The sight of the California peaks was now etched deeply in the mind of Padre Kino whose return to Dolores at Christmas reminded him of the successful expedition in Baja California nearly a decade before.

While California was still fresh on Kino's mind, he was joined in February by Juan Mateo Manje, the young nephew of Don Domingo Jironza Petris de Cruzat, who commanded the Flying Company of Sonora. Thus began a life long friendship between soldier and peacemaker. Now with Manje as escort, Kino again rode westward to the lands of Chief Soba in the lower Sonoran desert. This was basin and range country with vast stretches of mesquite, ironwood and creosote bushes, studded with saguaros and cholla. Rivers meandered out of the eastern hills during the

1694

rainy seasons, making travel circuitous but passable. This time Kino, Manje, and Padre Antonio Kappus struggled over the last few miles of waterless dunes to reach the shore itself. They had proven to themselves that they could reach the sea. Once acquainted with the distance to the Gulf and the intricacies of getting there, Manje shared Padre Kino's enthusiasm in building a craft to sail across the last barrier between them and California. Back at Dolores another expedition was organized in less than a month, and this time it would concentrate on building a boat they could drag to the mouth of the Río Concepción.

Kino's favorite Novena of Grace was finished by March 12; undoubtedly he pleaded for the intercession of St. Francis Xavier to bless these new ventures for the conversion of California. Then on March 16, the restless discoverers rode out of Dolores with a cavalcade of horses and pack animals laden with curved ribs, stays and spars for a small ship. Saws, axes, knives, nails, foodstuffs and trinkets completed the inventory of supplies. Winding down from the hill country onto the flat desert floor, the expedition lost no time along its route through Tubutama, Altar, and Pitiquito. Rains had left plentiful puddles of water and the desert was verdant with spring growth. From Manje's description of the trip, the two leaders were eyeing the location of suitable trees for timbers to construct the ship they had in mind. True to his apostolic temperament, Kino left the heavily burdened retinue to make its own way down the Río Altar while he road off to find yet more villages of potential converts. By the 21ˢᵗ they were at Caborca where they began immediate work on the boat. Lieutenant Manje, acting as construction boss, chose a towering cottonwood for the keel. He knew it wasn't the best wood for marine purposes, but it was all the region offered. Climbing into the upper branches, he attached ropes to guide the felling of the tree. Only he failed to stop the Indian laborers below who were vigorously sawing through the trunk. In an instant the thirty-eight foot tree toppled over smashing all its lower branches. In desperation the agile Manje clung to the trunk and miraculously survived the crash with neither broken bones or lesions! But he had enough of boat-building. In a few days he was off to explore places they had seen but not visited in February. Kino stayed behind to direct the roughing out of the keel and the cutting of other lumber for the rest of the boat. A week later, the hard-riding lieutenant was back with smoothed feathers and a bag of salt from Desemboque; it was time to return to the hill country.

Two months would pass before another expedition was formed; the wood that had been cut for the boat needed to dry before being shaped into ribs and planking. Enthusiastically, the two explorers set out for Tubutama where Padre Daniel Januske joyously received them. Kino moved on to Caborca while Manje probed the desert to the north. On this journey Manje first heard the Indians tell of a great river flowing westward near whose banks were tall and ancient houses. But that would have to wait until the boat was done. Crossing sixty miles of waterless desert, Manje rejoined Kino at Caborca on the night of June 11; nearly dead from thirst, the party had gulped contaminated water just before arriving and became violently ill for the next several days. Worse than their health was the letter that Kino clutched in his hand. Silently he let Manje read. Father Juan Muñoz de Burgos, the local Visitor, had forbidden Kino to continue building the boat. Although Kino had authority from the Provincial to do it, he humbly obeyed Muñoz who probably feared that the Tyrolese would sail over the horizon in his zeal to save California. The timbers were left to parch in the sun. For now, California was protected by an unbreachable Gulf.

Now terribly ill, Manje languished in the summer heat of Caborca, begging to be removed from this land of the burning sun. Scarcely able to eat or drink, Manje was given the last rites by his very distressed Jesuit companion. They had to get him back before he got even worse, so Indian servants carried him over a hundred miles in a litter on a trip that took six whole days. It fell to Father Campos at San Ignacio to cure the ailing soldier wracked by chills and fever. Having been refused a drink from a large jug in the mission, Manje stole through the night, probed the tank with a pole, and succeeded in overturning the huge *olla* that drenched him from head to toe. Soaked and embarrassed, the fever suddenly abated and Manje was cured. Was it the shock of cool water or the prayers of Padre Kino at Dolores?

NO MORE BOATS, ONLY BIG HOUSES

Whatever the illness was, Manje scurried off to San Juan Bautista to recuperate. Indian hostilities continued to threaten the frontier settlements, and the Spanish reaction was mounting. By November forces from Fronteras, Janos, and Sinaloa were joined for a campaign against the Apaches of the Gila. Having lost all his hair as a result of the fevers, Manje's general health had improved. He was back soldering as was his duty.

And Padre Kino? The Visitor had stopped Kino in his tracks. What he didn't know is that Manje had brought back the incredible news of a westward flowing river and big houses some eight days north of Caborca. If there was anything that sparked Kino's imagination, it was stories of far off peoples and places. While Manje recuperated at San Juan, the Padre of the Pimería tested the lieutenant's rumors. Inquiries were sent all over the north asking about the veracity of such claims. As the responses came back over the late summer, it was clearly evident that there was more here than vague rumor. But it would call for an expedition to the north. Kino's informants were visiting from San Xavier del Bac, and they would gladly guide him on a northerly expedition. The harvests were in and the weather had moderated, so by mid-November Padre Kino was again on the trail. Reaching San Xavier del Bac in short order, the cavalcade followed the meanders of the river past the craggy face of Picacho Peak to Piman villages situated on the south edges of the Río Gila. Rumors were right; these were extensively populated lands, and in Kino's opinion the native peoples were affable and industrious. The Pimería continued to be a land of much promise. Even more, he got word of other tribes to the west who spoke a very distinct language. That would mean yet another, longer trek down river. But he would have to keep that for another time.

As much as the Blackrobe had traveled in northern New Spain, no other archaeological ruin captured his imagination as much as the imposing walls of the great house, Casa Grande. Although he had never seen the impressive ancient city of Casas Grandes in Chihuahua, this soaring, thick walled citadel fit the descriptions he had heard so often from soldiers and missionaries stationed near those ruins. From the heights of the Casa Grande, others could be seen in the far distance, leading him to believe that his sector must have been that of the Seven Cities of Cíbola for which Coronado and Marcos de Niza had searched in vain. Moreover, this location fit into the contemporary notion about the migration of the Aztecs from the north to Mexico City. Why not? From here on the Gila, to Casas Grandes, to Mexico! At least it was sufficient justification to label an adjacent reservoir, Moctezuma's Tank. Kino's record of the ruins of Casa Grande became the first report by a European of such puzzling, crumbled cities in the desert. At the time of his historic visit, he also composed a vocabulary of the neighboring tribal languages and a map of the region, but, unfortunately, they have both been lost.

While Kino was away exploring the north country, big administrative changes blanketed the Pimería – Dolores and the fragile chain of missions stretching out into the desert were incorporated into a new rectorate. Since his arrival the Pima missions were a part of the rectorate of San Francisco Xavier, but the successful establishment and promise of more missions made a new administrative unit more attractive. Bureaucracy was not Kino's forte, so when he returned from the expedition to learn of the new rectorate, he was most content to congratulate Father Kappus of Cucurpe as the first rector. Let others push papers; let me ride under the starry skies!

Nuestra Señora de la Purísima Concepción de Caborca

New Men — New Missions

Almost eight years had sped past in the Pimería. Although a common impression has emerged that Kino was a lone missionary on a lonely frontier, nothing is further from the truth. True, Eusebio's enthusiasm and energy simply overwhelmed the "rim of Christendom" such that his companions on the frontier have been left in the dust of history. But following the visitation by Salvatierra, the Pimería Alta continually experienced the injection of new blood and a rapid circulation of assignments. The murder of Fathers Juan Ortíz Foronda and Manuel Sánchez in the Tarahumara had disrupted evangelization in the Sierra Madre; men had to be reassigned at least temporarily while peace was reestablished and missions rebuilt. The new rectorate of Dolores profited by an influx of missionaries to staff the inchoate missions at Tubutama, San Ignacio, and Cocóspera. Padre Antonio Arias at Tubutama was replaced by Daniel Janusque; Pedro Sandoval at Cocóspera by Juan Bautista Barli; Jorge Hostinski at San Ignacio, by Agustín de Campos; and the outpost of Nuestra Señora de la Concepción de Caborca would receive its first missionary in this expansion phase.

Kino had been very occupied with the harvests of '94. His maritime exploits were drying up in the desert heat when a young Sicilian, Padre Francisco Xavier Saeta, arrived in October, with orders from Father Visitor Burgos to be sent on to Caborca – this despite Kino's advice to the contrary. Once again Kino marshaled a parade of horses, cattle, and supplies to leave with Saeta at the remote mission with its small chapel and priest's house. At least Saeta was joyful in his new assignment and anxious to get started. Kino was anxious also to make his historic visit to Casa Grande as mentioned above. In his opinion, it would have been better to invite the vibrant young Italian along on the northern expedition and to introduce him to that expanding mission field. Caborca was many leagues into the western desert and the Pimas, as Manje had witnessed, were extremely discontent and unruly because of their treatment by Indian overseers at and around Tubutama. Caborca simply was unsafe, but it was not Kino's place to make the assignments.

Saeta's letters to Kino reveal traces of a strong, emerging friendship. The Sicilian radiated an enthusiasm to rival Kino's. He reflected Kino's own optimism that was still not blunted by opposition and rever-

1694

sals. Who knows but that the dried ribs and planks at Caborca might still be joined to make a boat that would bridge the gulf between the Pimería and California. Word from Saeta indicated that the fields were already giving promise of an abundant harvest which would come early in the warm desert air. So the new missionary planned a quick junket of the neighboring missions to beg more livestock, supplies, and some moments of companionship. Back again in Caborca, he found that Kino's handymen had finished a new corral and had completed a larger house for the priest. By early March Saeta was busily engaged in whitewashing the house with lime plaster; as isolated as the mission may have been, it would maintain a certain elegance! Rumors abounded that four Jesuits, companions of Saeta on the voyage from Spain, were in the vicinity. Might it be possible that they would assist in these new conversions? Saeta could only speculate and hope. What an Easter this would be!

Only he was unaware of the festering discontent at the mission of Tubutama, higher up the Río Altar. As Holy Week commenced, the cruelties of Antonio, the Opata overseer on the mission farm, brought about an explosive reaction. Already one Pima had died from a severe beating, and his relatives and friends vowed revenge. Catching Antonio in the pasture at dawn, they showered him with arrows. Although wounded, he managed to escape, hoping to reach the safety of the mission before he died. Although he reached the pueblo, he fell dead at the priest's house. Father Janusque himself, having learned of an imminent attack, had already ridden off to San Ignacio for help. Saeta, meanwhile in distant Caborca, blissfully attended to his gardening and the celebration of the season's special liturgies.

The sun rose gently over the near-by hills. It was Holy Saturday, April 2, 1695. Francisco Xavier Saeta was still thinking of the events of Good Friday as a band of determined Pimas approached his newly finished house. Exchanging a few pleasant greetings, he noted the surly responses and their menacing attitude. In an instant poisoned arrows thwacked into his chest; he staggered back into his room while dozens of arrows pierced him from all sides. The joy of Easter was being splattered with the blood of the first martyr of the Pimería Alta. His body crumpled on the floor as he clutched the figure of the slain Jesus which had been so much a part of the previous day's celebrations. An irony and a tragedy.

Indian runners from Caborca dashed to find Padre Kino. Word of the murder reached him in hours. What he had so feared many months before had happened – distant and defenseless, there had been no way to warn or protect him. And then, Indian messengers, who came by a different route, handed him Saeta's last letters. On the outside of one, Saeta had scrawled news of the rebellion at Tubutama and a plea: "Dear Father, don't lose sight of me." It was already too late.

Caborca, Oquitoa, and Tubutama smoldered in ruins. San Ignacio and Cocóspera were exposed to attack. What others had always predicted was happening; the Pimería Alta, once peaceful and filled with promise, was in revolt. Yet, not all the Indians were involved; peace still might have a chance to work. As soon as word reached General Domingo Jironza at San Juan, an expeditionary force of Spaniards and loyal Indian auxiliaries set out for Caborca. It was a tragic scene. Saeta's body was partially cremated. The ashes were carried to Cucurpe for burial, and the articulated statue of the crucified Christ to which Saeta had clung in death was sent on to Arispe. Although the funeral for the martyred Christians was impressive, it could not offset the sorrow and resentment that remained strong in everyone's mind. Such episodes almost always invited a stinging reaction from the Spanish settlers. Jironza dispatched his erstwhile lieutenant, Antonio de Solís, to hunt down the murderers and exact punishment. In a matter of days he terrorized several Piman villages. Just knowing that Solís had been commissioned to regain control jangled Kino's nerves because this military officer had done more to unsettle peace in the Pimería than any other single official. His reputation for swift and severe punishment hung over the territory like the angel of death. So Kino moved quickly to mobilize his friends among the Indian leaders; perhaps he could avert a catastrophe.

TREACHERY BEFORE A TRUCE

Within a few short weeks the Sobaipuri and Soba chiefs identified and located those responsible for the murder of Saeta and the Christian Indians at the missions. Solís had wasted little time in reprisals among unsuspecting Indian rancherías. The Pimas knew they had to sue for peace or face decimation at the hands of a relentless Spanish cavalry. With Kino's good offices, a meeting was arranged at El Tupo, a village clearing just west of Magdalena. For three days bands of Indians converged on the clearing of the ciénega nearby. Solís and his light horse cavalry milled about in anticipation. On the morning of June 9 the Indian leaders decided to hand over some of those who had participated in the revolt. The chief perpetrators were still in hiding. By agreement the Indians left their weapons stashed in the bosque and entered the clearing unarmed

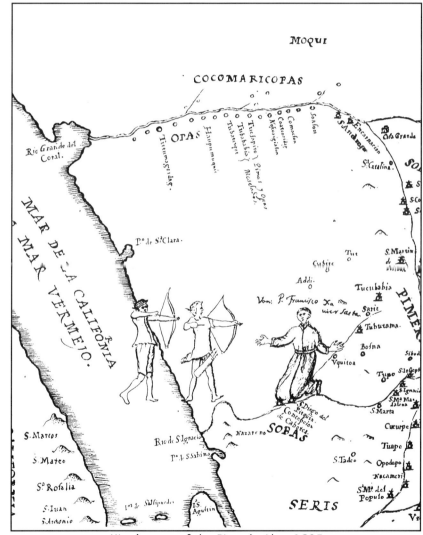

Kino's map of the Pimería Alta, 1695

for the impromptu trial. Sitting on the damp earth in a circle, they waited. Soon a neighboring chief dragged one of the ringleaders to his feet, proclaiming his guilt to Lt. Solís. Surrounded by his armed cavalrymen, Solís drew his saber. For a moment it glinted in the morning sun; then it swished through the air, toppling the Indian's head into the trampled weeds! Justice ala Solís.

In total panic, the Indians, guilty as well as innocent, lurched to their feet and lunged in the direction of their stacked weapons. This was no trial. It was a trap. Musket fire cracked from soldiers seated on their horses, and swords flashed through the smoke as the Spanish cavalry cut down the terror-stricken Indians. In a matter of minutes the council of El Tupo was ended. The ciénega ran deep in the blood of the simple people who had trusted too much. And from that day forward, the marshy ground has been known as La Matanza, the place of the massacre.

Kino couldn't believe his eyes. The wailing of the wounded, the choked cries of the dying, the blood, the terror, the treachery made him sick to death. In the days to come he could never forget the murder of his Indian friends before his own eyes. And he fought back the memories of that day in La Paz twelve years before when innocent and unsuspecting natives were blown away by violence that some insisted was the best kind of schooling for Christian morality. Kino and Campos left the scene grief-stricken, angry, and determined to turn back the tides of war. But what could two Blackrobes do in a desolate desert to unseat the arrogance of power?

The frontier exploded into open war for three terror-filled months. The ponderous Spanish cavalry struck fear into the Indians, but their warriors continued to dart from mountain strongholds to burn missions and fields, escaping long before the Spaniards could react. The "hawks" who put their trust in power made no progress toward peace. Frustrated and irritated by their failure, they handed the problem over to Kino whose friends their justice had murdered. And typically, Padre Eusebio accepted the responsibility of bringing peace back to the Pimería. With assurances from the beloved Blackrobe the Piman leaders summoned their people once again to a council of peace —and symbolically the site of La Matanza at Tupo was chosen for the rendezvous. This time, however, a genuine treaty of peace was agreed upon, and the site's bloody name was changed to "Santa Rosa" because it was on the August feast day of that saint the documents were signed. One priest did in days what confounded the agents of the Crown for months.

ON TO MEXICO CITY

One might expect that after the Pimería had calmed down that Padre Kino, now fifty years old, would relax somewhat himself. But no. In November, only three months after the peace was effected, Kino was in the saddle. This time his destination was Mexico City! The 1200 mile ride was completed in seven weeks; riding at his side were the sons of his chieftain friends who were as astonished at the riches of Mexico as the Mexican officials were at the stalwart young Pimans. His visit was by no means to renew old acquaintances; he rode on urgent business — to press for the reopening of the California missions and to explain what was really happening on the frontier. Part of the Padre's explanation was made through the pages of a small book he wrote about the martyrdom of Saeta. His untimely and tragic death provided an occasion for Kino to clarify the situation in the Pimería and to elaborate on his own mission methods. Kino knew he was fighting for his missionary life be cause ugly rumors had en-snared both the man and his work. Quite unbeknown to Kino while he rode back to Mexico, there was a move-ment to have him removed and stationed at the Jesuit university. So he unleashed all the talent he had in writ-ing and drawing maps.

He really did not need to demonstrate his ample literary prowess, how-ever, since Kino's plight had

Jesuit Novitiate at Tepozotlán

come to the attention of the Jesuit General Tirso González in Rome. Comparing Kino to St. Francis Xavier, the powerful head of the order made it scathingly clear to the superiors in New Spain that Kino was not to be hindered in his extraordinary efforts in the Pimería. Shortly before Kino arrived in the capital, a letter from the General reached the new Provincial, Father Juan de Palacios, indicating that Kino should be assigned to six months in the Pimería and six months in California. Rome recognized the missionary's apostolic restlessness as a virtue!

1696

In fact, the very afternoon of Kino's arrival, January 8, 1696, Father Juan María Salvatierra joined him at the Casa Profesa where they renewed their friendship and reaffirmed their mutual interest in California. With the new authorization from the General, Kino could press for a return to the peninsula, if only the Viceroy could be convinced. And that became the immediate task of these two holy conspirators. Salvatierra enlisted the aid of Father Juan de Ugarte, a giant of a man and an accomplished solicitor. Between the three of them a plan for the conversion of California was concocted that would have repercussions for centuries to come. It was the birth of the Pious Fund of the Californias – but more on that later.

Padre Kino had lost none of his ability to argue a good case. The Provincial agreed to send five new men to the Pimería so the expansion could continue apace. Then, having spent exactly one month in Mexico City, the Padre was back in the saddle and headed homeward. As always, Kino's routes were circuitous, this time taking him via Durango where he met up with another priest destined for work in the Pimería. Easter was spent in celebratory fashion at Conicari, and then he headed into the mountain country to see Father Horatio Polici, the new visitor. From his own memoirs we learn that despite all the seeming misfortunes and setbacks dealt him by Providence, Kino was being favored all the while. Near Oputo the very military escort he traveled with through terrain ravaged by Jocomes was ambushed and wiped out to a man; that is, all except Padre Kino who had made one of his typical brief detours to greet two old Jesuit companions.

News of his arrival at Dolores in mid May, 1696, swept through the mission territory. The whole of the Pimería surged to life. Chiefs of distant tribes walked scores and hundreds of miles to celebrate with him at Dolores. The Indian residents of Cosari and their visitors joined together to harvest the winter wheat in the fertile valleys. Many who had been instructed earlier were baptized; others had to wait because they were not sufficiently prepared. Rarely, if ever, did Padre Eusebio let his enthusiasm outrun his responsibilities. In a way this return was a miniature copy of what Kino's original coming to the Pimería had meant. The events of the summer manifested unity, friendship, industry, gaiety, and plenty revolving around a common sacramental life in the mission pueblo. What had been words in writing the life of Saeta were now deeds in the desert.

CRITICS CHURN THE RUMOR MILL

However, the years immediately following the Pima uprising of 1695 were turbulent ones for Padre Kino. The missions had to be rebuilt, confidence restored, and factions abolished. The policies of the pastor of Dolores were not too popular with some of the other missionaries in the region, especially with Father Francisco Xavier Mora, the Puebla born rector of the district of Dolores. He was heady with power, and when Padre Kino returned, he felt threatened by every shadow. In a matter of months he and Kino were embroiled in a bitter fight over punishing the Piman murders of Saeta – a crime that had gone unpunished since Kino's trip to Mexico. Pens flared in accusation, and faces blushed with embarrassment and shock. Kino was simply not the unthinking "dead stick" Mora thought he should be. Mora's stodgy asceticism smacked of ideology and unreality. "Kino's fame was too great" – especially among the Indians. That would really never do if the man were to be a humble religious. Nothing, however, really fazed Padre Kino. He dealt as bluntly with his accusers as he did forthrightly in behalf of his Indian dependents. The Pimería was shaping up just as rapidly as before.

While Kino's critics fussed and fumed, he tirelessly drove herds of cattle and sheep into the San Pedro and Santa Cruz valleys in preparation for a whole new string of missions. He was counting on the Provincial's promise of four or five new men for the expanding frontier. In four separate entradas, averaging nearly 200 miles each, he was making it clear that he was serious about a permanent shift of the mission frontier to the north. And at fifty-two years of age, his inexhaustible vigor peeved some of his confreres – particularly the younger Mora, his Rector at Arispe.

In May, 1697, the hard-riding Padre was scarcely out of the saddle when a dispatch reached Dolores from Father Palacios, the Mexican Provincial: Kino was to be reassigned

San Miguel de Oposura (Moctezuma)

to California! The Crown had accepted the Kino-Salvatierra proposal to christianize California exclusive of any royal assistance. The new missionaries even held the unusual power to control both naval and military units sent to protect the missions. It was the answer to a dream. And it even thrilled Father Mora to think that the troublesome Kino would be gone for good!

But one man's dream is another man's night-mare. What would become of the Pimería without Padre Eusebio? The news of the transfer was one of good riddance to Mora; it was unthinkable to Padre Horacio Polici, the Visitor at Oposura; it appeared catastrophic to General Jironza at San Juan and the governor at Parral. Frantic letters from the north blew into Mexico City in a storm of protest. Pity the poor Provincial! One month Kino is damned by Dame Rumor and the next, deified by civil magistrates.

And what about Kino? He knew he was being stretched on the rack of obedience- with his feet in the Pimería and his head in California. While the irascible tug-of-war over his destiny was taking place, Kino calmly wrote Father General Tirso González asking to spend six months in each place. He would rather divide his time than his torso. But one thing even Kino had to admit – somehow the colonials had come to appreciate the incalculable influence of this pioneer Padre. They may have obstructed him in earlier days, but now they needed his presence.

Padre Mora, the budding scrooge of the Sonora valley, scoffed that Kino had contrived the whole, mass protest! The juice from Mora's own sour-grapes mentality mixed into the ink that penned the best refutation ever to the opposition to Padre Kino.

While couriers on horseback raced the wheels of fate, Kino complied with his orders and left Dolores, the mission he founded ten years before. He rode down the San Miguel and across the scorching flatland toward the Río Yaqui where Padre Salvatierra was awaiting his arrival. Soon the California adventure would begin all over again. The desert can be a lonely place, particularly when one has just been turned out of the land to which have been given years of one's life. Padre Eusebio wasn't sad, though; in fact, he wasn't even looking back. Perhaps he should have been – because a courier galloped after him wreathed in swirling dust. Finally overtaking the Padre, the messenger displayed new and special orders from the Provincial in Mexico. Kino was to return to the Pimería, as the Viceroy himself had ordered, because the government and the people needed him here and not in California!

In the life of Padre Eusebio Francisco Kino this was the moment of final fulfillment. There would be no more reversals because the pattern of his work was set. He was destined to be poised between two worlds. His new orders committed him to the Pimería but only on the assumption that Sonora and Arizona would be a base of operations. His missions had to be forged into an agricultural empire that would sustain the bleakest of California years. Now his explorations would have to seek out new ports on the Gulf. His own life would be spent more in the saddle than the sanctuary.

It is said that mountains rise highest where valleys course deepest. The loss of Kino to the Pimería had cut a chasm into the hopes of the Indians, but his announced return propelled them back to newer heights. Warriors and chieftains, women and children converged on the good Padre of Dolores. Now they felt confident in pressing their requests since the loyal champion of their cause had come back. Kino sensed the tempo and channeled all energies into a giant pilgrimage to Baserac, to the feet of the Father Visitor. Some Indians had traveled well over 200 miles to join in the welcome. Why not transform their hopes into a pilgrimage of petition? The triumphant and confident column tramped right through Arispe where Padre Mora could witness the growing popularity of his "problem" Padre. Through canyons and over rugged mountain passes the pilgrims went — through Oposura, Guasavas, right to Padre Horacio Polici. The peace march won its point: more missionaries were promised, and soldiers, too, for a new garrison at Quiburi.

Salvatierra had been waiting on the shores of the Gulf for the arrival of the highly experienced royal cosmographer; he would know as well as anyone what lay ahead on the distant "island." But Kino's orders had changed and Salvatierra was on his own to launch the newest attempt to christianize the Californias. And Kino? With characteristic enthusiasm, he covered over the bitter disappointment of his sudden reassignment and plunged headlong into a vigorous new mission expansion. While Salvatierra's fragile fleet battled the winds and waves to California, Kino was conducting his parade of petition to Bacerac. On October 6, "the feast of Our Lady of the Rosary" Kino piously lied, he prayed for Salvatierra who would soon found the new mission of Loreto in Baja California. You see, October 6 is the feast of San Bruno when Kino's last valiant attempt to settle California was begun; it is only the vigil of the Rosary, but he wanted the record to dissimulate his disappointment and to place himself in the patronage of the Virgin.

A NEW ERA OPENS

With Padre Polici's blessing and encouragement, Kino's next expedition left Dolores on November 2, 1697, opening a new era for the Pimería. Unlike previous expeditions to the north, this one had a fresh purpose – the sustenance of California by land and sea. Padre Kino, Manje, and ten Indians led a well provisioned pack train northeast past Remedios, Cocóspera, and Suamca. They threaded the Huachuca Mountains and finally camped at Santa Cruz de Gaybanepitea. Close on their trail came Captain Cristóbal Martin Bernal and twenty-two dragoons from the presidio of Fronteras. On the 9th, the combined groups rode into Quiburi and greeted Chief Coro of the Sobaipuri nation who were in the midst of celebrating a victory over their hostile neighbors, the Jocomes and Janos. Seeing scalps and hearing the tales of combat, the Spaniards, who had been skeptical of Sobaipuri valor, joined in the wild festivities and merriment. It's always a cause for joy when one's allies demonstrate strength and effectiveness.

From Quiburi the men of the Cross and the Crown, accompa-

1697

nied now by Coro and thirty braves, continued down the San Pedro valley. The column's route knifed between friend and foe because the eastern slope of the river was Apache country. Apparently the sting of defeat was still strong, however, for they encountered only friends. The expedition reached the junction of the San Pedro and Gila rivers and turned westward to search out the large ruins in the sprawling desert. Since Manje had first heard rumors of the great abandoned cities, this had been a prime attraction for Kino's curiosity. The fascination of the great mystery surrounding the disappearance of the ancient tribes who built the great houses and aqueducts along the Gila bit deeply into the Spanish adventurers. It was eerie to be so alone where there had once been such vast human occupation.

Braving stormy winds and rain the expedition bivouacked beside the ruins of the Casa Grande where Padre Kino, who had fasted all day, celebrated Mass. It was Monday, November 18, 1697. The Sobaipuris

Ruins of Casa Grande

talked about an ancient chief named Ciba (the Bitter One) who had ruled these vanished peoples until they abandoned the cities and their huge aqueducts to go south east. Perhaps, the Spaniards thought, these were the precursors of Moctezuma! After all, the legends said that the Aztecs came from the north to Mexico. Viewing the thick walled ruins like a field engineer, Manje felt it would be possible to be re-roofed and to clean out the rooms for a useful visita or military outpost. He sketched the imposing building into the margin of his journal.

The next day Padre Kino pushed on as far as San Andrés, the old Tudacson, near modern Sacatón. Indians stained with red pigment stirred Manje's curiosity because a young warrior described the paint in a way that smacked of "quicksilver." What a boon a new mercury mine would mean to the silver industry of the north! With their interests slaked by new discoveries, the expedition reluctantly turned back toward the

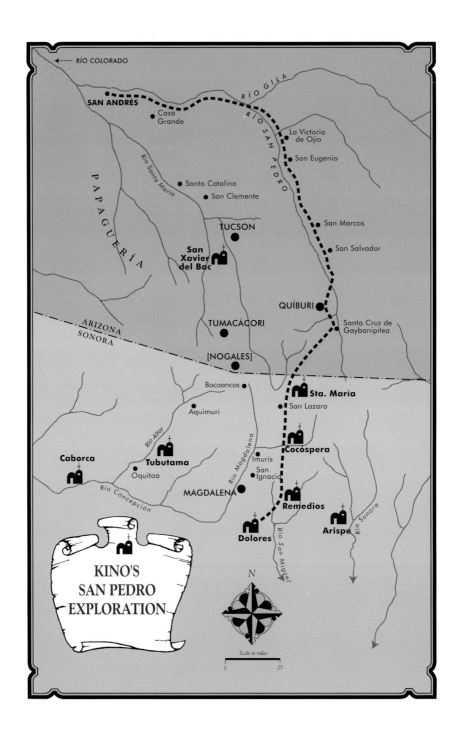

RÍO COLORADO

RÍO GILA

RÍO SAN PEDRO

SAN ANDRÉS

Casa Grande

La Victoria de Ojio

San Eugenio

Río Santa María

Santa Catalina

San Clemente

P A P A G U E R Í A

San Marcos

TUCSON

San Salvador

San Xavier del Bac

QUÍBURI

ARIZONA
SONORA

TUMACÁCORI

Santa Cruz de Gaybanipitea

[NOGALES]

Bocoancos

Aquimuri

Sta. María

San Lazaro

Río Altar

Cocóspera

Caborca

Tubutama

Río Magdalena

Imuris

San Ignacio

Óquitoa

Río Concepción

MAGDALENA

Remedios

Río Sonora

Dolores

Arispe

Río San Miguel

KINO'S
SAN PEDRO
EXPLORATION

N

Scale in miles

0   25

62

Santa Cruz river trail and home. Everyone was elated with the success of the entrada. Kino saw a new peace being born of Sobaipuri strength; Manje felt it was a step toward the reduction of the nations of North America; and the Indians were thrilled by the hearty interest shown in them by the white men from the south.

Since the first visit of Chief Humari to Dolores two years before, the idea of weaving a defensive alliance among the Sobaipuris attracted the attention of regional Spanish officials. Kino's expeditions, at the behest of Father Visitor Polici, proved the validity of the concept and confirmed the loyalty of the Indian tribes. The Apaches were contained by the Pimería's solid wall of defense. Now both missionaries and military men could turn their backs on the eastern frontier. The "tierra incognita" to the west spread before them in all its baffling expanse and hazy rumor. Far-ranging hunters spoke of distant peoples, giant rivers, and even armored white men riding antlered animals. Padre Eusebio's home mission of Dolores had suddenly ceased to be the heart of the Pimería because his mission borders were hurtling westward. Pimas, Papagos, Sobas, Cocomaricopas, Opas, and Yumas – all the tribes of the desert west would grow accustomed to the dust clouds of Padre Kino's pack trains. He was a restless man of peace, pushing a four hundred mile frontier farther into the unknown.

THE EXPEDITIONS OF '98 AND '99

Except for the usual array of detractors, most of the leaders in the Pimeria Alta were enthused with Kino's discoveries. Even the military complement that had accompanied him accomplished much more than they had ever been able to do on their own. The Blackrobe's non-threatening manner quickly created a sense of trust among the Indians who responded knowledgeably to his inquiries about trails, pasture, and water. Obviously, diplomacy worked better than a musket or a lance!

1698

Help was now on its way. Padre Gaspar de Barillas, formerly at Arispe, was transferred to the rectorate of Dolores. Once again on the trail with Manje and his successor, Juan Sarmiento, Kino introduced Barillas to the missions of the western desert. He chose Caborca which had remained vacant since the martyrdom of Saeta. But the Pimeria remained exposed to Apache attacks and rumors of unrest, such that Barillas only lasted at Caborca through June and July. Without doubt, the Pimeria was experiencing continual turbulence that threatened peace and stability. It wasn't the Pimas as much as the Jocomes who were responsible. Finally, in April, Chief Coro and his men assisted the Spanish forces by soundly defeating the Apache chief Capotcari in hand to hand combat.

It was the fall of 1698 before Kino was able to mount another major expedition. The earlier months of the year had seen the tragic plundering of Cocóspera by the Apaches, the swift and savage retaliation captained by the Piman, Coro, and a resumption of boat-building at Caborca. By September, although still weak and tired from various illnesses and verbally sparring with Padre Mora, Padre Kino took a new captain, Diego Carrasco, and seven faithful Indians on a reconnaissance of the "great river," the Gila. He fully intended to scale the Sierra Estrella but fever cut him down and he languished for some days at San Andrés. Although his intentions were to survey the Gulf coast from the heights of the Estrellas, the natives explained to him that the Gila flowed around these mountains and emptied into the Gulf far to the southwest!

Partially recuperated but stunned by the news about the course

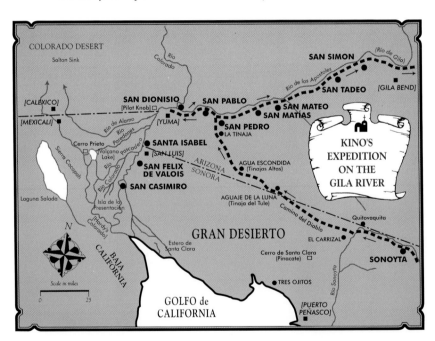

of the Gila, Padre Kino and Carrasco wheeled the pack train southward and cut across the heart of Papaguería. Listening to the Indian reports, they knew the trail to the Gulf would be treacherous, but they were determined to accomplish the purpose of the entrada. The Indians at Sonoita directed the explorers toward Pinacate Peak. Kino climbed its volcanic ridges to see the Gulf coast arching away to the west at today's Adair Bay. He had been wrong about the northern limits of the Gulf waters. Furthermore, the Gila emptied into another great river somewhere to the north and west. From Pinacate, or Santa Clara as it was then called, they turned back and took a shorter and more direct route home through Caborca where fresh supplies and mounts awaited them.

The pace of the trip was typical for Kino. He had traveled some eight hundred miles in slightly more than three weeks. During the trip he took time out to baptize nearly 400 infants, instruct others in the faith, and acquaint himself with hundreds of destitute Papagos in the arid land.

After a three month rest at Dolores Padre Eusebio enlisted the aid of Padre Adam Gilg and Captain Manje on a new entrada into the Papaguería. There was nothing scanty about this expedition: he assembled ninety pack animals, eighty horses, thirty-six head of cattle, eight loads of provisions, and a host of Indian vaqueros! Whatever lay to the west, Sonoita was certainly a key, and he meant to establish a new mission ranch there to serve as a base camp for the northwest explorations. The massive column picked up even more supplies from faithful Padre Agustín de Campos at San Ignacio and moved around the hills into the Altar valley. They cut a little westward along the southern flanks of the Baboquivari Mountains and camped near the weird peak that dominates the range and the desert vistas. In nine days, on the 16th of February, 1699, they reached Sonoita and prepared for the death-defying crossing of the Camino del Diablo.

1699

The Devil's Highway is one of those ancient trails that even modern man has not reopened. Its route lies along a jagged, parched path from water tank to water hole. The thrust into the desert missed the first promised water; it was almost as if the devil himself were welcoming the explorers. They rode into the night and finally reached a granite tank glistening in the moonlight. Kino and Manje called it Moon Tank, in memory of their midnight discovery. Surrounded by desolate hills and dry plains they scurried from aguaje to aguaje – Tinajas Altas to Dripping Springs. In four days of hard riding they covered more than 125 miles and finally arrived at the thirst quenching waters of the "Río Grande," the Gila. Exhausted from their adventures along the Camino

del Diablo, Kino, Gilg, and Manje rested at a Yuman village just east of the Gila Range where the river turns north before slicing through to the Colorado; they called it San Pedro.

The morning after arriving at the Gila a hundred Yumans padded up the river trail to offer the newcomers gifts and words of welcome. Manje was anxious to go down river, but Kino sensed it would be better to postpone further penetration.

Moon Tanks on the Devil's Highway

There was something astonishing about Kino's sensitivities to Indian protocol. But Manje managed to satisfy his curiosity by riding to a peak in the Gila mountain range from which he saw the junction of the two great rivers, the Gila and the Colorado. No more could the Gila be misnamed the "Río Grande," because the mighty Colorado made the Gila look like a creek. While recouping their strength and that of the animals, Indians from the Colorado valley brought gifts in exchange for trinkets offered them by the Spanish exploring party. Among them were some curious and beautiful blue shells that Kino recognized as coming only from the "opposite" shores of the Pacific. These shells turned out to be far more significant than mere souvenirs!

When the trio left San Pedro, at the suggestion of Padre Gilg, the Gila was renamed the "Río de los Apostoles," and the Indian villages along the river were each named in a litany of the other apostles as the party moved up river. Reaching the great bend of the Gila, they struck across the desert and negotiated a pass through the Sierra Estrella which deposited them near the now familiar village of San Andrés de Coata. What a marvel Padre Kino must have been to the Pimas who watched this man in his mid-fifties pop out of the desert every few months coming almost always from a different direction!

Once again at Dolores, almost in time for the celebration of the Novena of Grace (March 2-12), word traveled throughout the province that Padre Kino was back from lands of fabled riches. Then, a whole summer was spent in crossing epistolary swords over the worth of vast desert lands accruing to Spain from Kino's explorations. Cynical colonists couldn't see the potential of the land or the people northwest of the Pimería; Kino was "making insects look like elephants and painting grandeurs in Pima Land which did not exist there." Salvatierra, of course, was delighted and encouraged that there might be some new routes to California and he invited Kino again to join in a maritime exploration – but superiors were still fearful of letting Kino get too close to his former mission.

During the last week of October, 1699, Padre Antonio Leal, the new Visitor, and Padre Francisco Gonzalvo, joined Kino and Manje on a new entrada which was scheduled this time to reach the juncture of the Gila and the Colorado. The entourage had decided to rendezvous at San Xavier del Bac before setting off for the net work of rivers to the northwest. But Captain Cristóbal Bernal sent word that the military escort under his command was being diverted to assist Chief Coro in a campaign against the hostile Jocomes. Then, two of Padre Leal's attendants fell ill while waiting at Bac. A change of plan was imperative because a deep penetration into unknown territory without military escort might prove too risky. Not wishing to disappoint Leal, Kino and Manje chose to cross the Papaguería to demonstrate the friendliness and extent of these lands which would help to put the lie to the critics of expansion. With the impatience of seasoned adventurers Kino and Manje dashed from village to village baptizing infants and the sick and reassuring the natives of their interest and commitment. The desert seemed to spring to life for the Padre Visitor since hundreds of Indians poured into each pueblo along the route. It may have been a disappointment not to have attempted the trek to the Yumans, but it was a welcome reward to see that Padre Kino was correct in his assessment of the Pima and Papago nations.

While Padres Leal and Gonzalvo jostled wearily along the desert trails, Padre Eusebio and Captain Juan Mateo were undertaking a kind of "flying mission." In the five days they were separated from the main cavalcade, the pair rode over three hundred miles throughout the territory adjoining the main trail. Kino preached and baptized; Manje counted heads for the Crown. Apparently the main body moved faster than they anticipated, because the last day and night out Kino and Manje churned through fifty leagues of desert wash and cholla forest! They caught Leal and Gonzalvo at Búsanic, slept four hours, and then rose early to butcher some livestock, distribute presents, and hold a civil ceremony to appoint justices. No wonder Leal and Gonzalvo were glad to get back to Dolores and rest.

But Kino wasn't in the mood to rest. Something had been bothering him since the trip to the lower Gila. He kept thinking about the simple, precious gift the sturdy Yumans had given him at San Pedro – those blue abalone shells. At the time he had smiled and thanked the natives, but perforce he had to concentrate on his explorations and survival. It was on the return ride when Padre Kino was reminiscing beneath the winter sun that the salty breeze and crashing surf of Baja California thundered in his memory. Those shells were seen by him only once, fifteen years before on the mapping expedition to the "opposite shore" of the Isla de California! Could there be a connection? Possibly, but not probably. On previous trips, especially to the volcanic peak of Santa Clara (Pinacate), he had seen through his telescope that the coast line veered westward, but he suspected a narrow sea passage still led to the northwest separating the mainland from the Californias. That's just the way Kino drew it on his "Teatro" map of 1695. But now doubts were growing on the basis of new evidence.

BLUE SHELLS — A BOTHER OR A BOON?

Padre Kino witnessed the turn of the 18th century at Dolores. His work load was heavy and the new California missions under Salvatierra were needing increased assistance. The thrust to the Colorado just meant more work and Dolores was too far away for such involvements as establishing visitas on the Gila and the Colorado. Nor was any new blood being pumped into the Pimería these days. Life was settling into a predictable, hectic routine. That is, until March. While Padre Eusebio was at Remedios, a chieftain from the Gila Pimas arrived with news of the

1700

68

river peoples and a cross strung with twenty blue shells, a gift from the governor of the Cocomaricopas. The cross was accepted with graciousness, but once again the shells made the Padre uneasy. The unanswered question of their origin nagged at his scientific nature.

A partial solution to the problem of expansion would be to build a mission closer to these new fields of labor, so Padre Kino chose the fertile and extensive ranchería of Bac to become the base for future northwestern entradas. The blue-shell question simmered for a few weeks, and then began to plague him for an answer. With Easter season now over, he set out in late April with ten Indian friends – destination: the Gila pueblos. On the way he would attend to new construction at Remedios and Cocóspera, which was being renovated after its disastrous sacking in 1697. However, news overtook the cavalcade that a contingent of cavalry had ridden into the western desert because of troubles in Soba country. Alone and without escort, it seemed to Kino that a change in plan might be more prudent, so he pulled up at San Xavier del Bac. With the question of the shells very much on his mind, he decided to send out inquiries about the origins of the blue shells. Runners went north, west and even east to call the great chiefs to a "Blue Shell Conference" at Bac. In a matter of days the Padre's messages got a response; chiefs and couriers came with the certain information that the blue shells from the Yumans could not have come from the Gulf because the blue-crusted abalone didn't occur in those dense waters. They had been traded hand to hand from the distant Pacific.

Abalone Shells

While waiting for the replies, Kino devoted his time to instructing the Sobaipuris in the catechism, and, true to his nature, he directed the laying of foundations for a large church. April 28 was the unforgettable day for the beginning of the church that has since transformed itself into an international memorial. As for Padre Kino, it was time to petition Father Visitor Leal for a permanent transfer to Bac which would place him much closer to the new mission field. He saddled up and rode south toward Dolores with a whole new future on his mind. At dawn on May 3, Kino was preparing to say Mass at San Cayetano de Tumacácori when

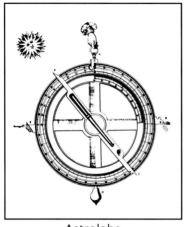
Astrolabe

he was handed a letter from Father Campos at San Ignacio. It was an urgent summons for him to intervene in the scheduled execution, May 4, of a prisoner in the custody of the soldiers. Riding until midnight, he rested at Imuris, reaching San Ignacio at sunrise – just in time to celebrate Mass and save a poor Piman from death. Such was Kino's whole life in the saddle – long treks in the desert, rapid rides in the cause of justice and mercy, and tedious journeys bringing food and supply to distant Indian tribes; there was no casual rest for the Apostle to the Pimas.

No sooner was Kino back at Dolores than word came from Leal that permission was granted for the transfer to Bac – he only needed to wait for a replacement, a replacement that never ever came. With confidence and expectation at that time Kino dispatched seven hundred head of livestock to start the mission farms at Bac, and he set about making plans for an expedition to the Colorado in the early fall. Everyone was enthusiastic about the prospects of the new missions to the northwest with San Xavier del Bac as the central staging area. Letters were sent off to Salvatierra in distant California about his conviction that there had to be a land passage to those new missions – and a note of encouragement for Salvatierra to join in a fall expedition after harvest and before the annual round-up.

TO THE COLORADO — FINALLY

The summer heat had abated; the rains had drenched the desert, and it was opportune to cross the once burning desert. On September 24, 1700, he left Dolores – destination, the juncture of the Gila and the Colorado. This time he took a direct route to reach the big bend of the Gila by crossing the Papaguería. With ten servants and sixty pack animals he wound his way through Remedios, Síboda, Búsanic, and Tucubavia. By the 30th they had reached Nuestra Señora de Merced del Batqui where Kino split the cavalcade in two, sending the majority of the pack animals and horses westward to San Marcelo de Sonidag (Sonoita) to await his return via the Camino del Diablo. He had learned on earlier trips how to negotiate the difficult, waterless wastes. Striking north-northwest to the famous painted rocks of Gila Bend, Kino arrived at El Tutto where Indian messengers had gathered to greet him and bring news of recent victories over marauding Apaches. By sending more than half his retinue to San Marcelo, he had placed constraints on both his route of return and the time he had left to reach the Colorado. But Kino felt himself to be in the element he loved so much, to be under the open skies and meeting new peoples. Every day down stream meant a night spent talking and instructing friendly new Indians; it was hard on his schedule, but it satisfied his sense of apostolate. He had come to the New World to preach the Gospel and eager ears were listening.

On the 7th of October half his allotted time was exhausted. Teaching and baptizing had taken its toll, and anxiety about a return lurked in the back of his mind. Once again, he had neither reached the Colorado nor seen the headlands of California. So this time Kino climbed a small range of hills to view the land with a long range telescope. There was no sea in sight, just expanses of land cut by the meanders of the two huge rivers. The sight was enough for Kino. He concluded that he had seen the lands of California. And his Indian companions were weary of these explorations and uncomfortable because they had hard work to do in rounding up livestock at their villages. It was time to turn back.

The Pimas were relieved when Kino agreed. But then, in the slanting shadows of the afternoon a band of Yumas caught up with Padre Kino insisting that he come to visit their villages on the river. If he didn't postpone the return, he was certain to offend the sensitive and powerful Yuman people. It was a double dilemma between time and fright. Tossing caution to the winds and letting his customary optimism be his guide, Padre Eusebio smiled at the persistent, tearful Indians and agreed to go to their village on the Colorado. He rose before dawn, celebrated Mass and cantered down river, coming across clusters of Indians who had traveled through the night to meet him on the trail. His mule's gait slowed with each mile as the welcoming throng grew. By noon he rode into the huge Yuma town where over a thousand Indians greeted him in peace. Within another day some five hundred more arrived and word came that hundreds were on their way from north and south along the Colorado!

The Yumas were gigantic in stature, and one of them was the largest Indian Kino had ever seen. It must have been a little nerve-wracking to be the willing captive of such giants. But Padre Kino's own good will and understanding of the Indian ways won a whole new nation in friendship. Staying overnight, he taught and preached under the stars;

Kino Peak, Southern Arizona

truly the desert had become his cathedral. Early the next morning on the feast of San Dionisio he christened two sickly adults, naming one after the martyr-patron. Since his duties at Dolores beckoned, he had to leave, but he promised a return – soon.

Prodding his mule, Kino found a fresh relay waiting for him at Las Sandias. He immediately turned south along the arid Camino del Diablo toward Sonoita. He knew the location of the hidden tanks and rode with assurance that they would find water. And again, typical of his explorer's instinct, he sent the relay team ahead to find pasture and take a siesta, while he trotted up a distant hill to view the sprawling lands of the Colorado delta. Still no sign of the sea. He overtook the others and by sunset arrived at the Tinaja de la Luna (Moon Tank). After a brief respite they rode for three more hours in order to make the next morning's ride to Carrizal easier and more pleasant. By eight o'clock on October 12, the exploratory party reached San Marcelo – tired from the trip but almost on time. Among experienced travelers along that stretch of desert, Kino's prowess was olympic. The devil himself must have been grumbling as Kino turned his trail of death into a highway of conquest.

Eight days later at Dolores there was rejoicing to see everyone back safely. Kino lost no time in broadcasting letters to his Jesuit companions and Spanish officials. There was a land route to the Californias. Now all that remained was to make the crossing which would promise to be a logistical nightmare. On his desk was a letter from Salvatierra, written the previous August and telling him of the great need they had for food and supplies because no ship had come from Mexico for fourteen months!

KINO AND SALVATIERRA ON THE TRAIL TOGETHER

Padre Juan María Salvatierra in the meanwhile had not been idle. His new mission at Loreto in Baja California desperately needed supplies from the mainland. So the industrious missionary crossed the Gulf in late December, 1700 to secure provisions in Sinaloa. In January he scouted the harbor of Guaymas for a new mission and seaport site which would be more efficient to supply California than the older port on the Río Yaqui. Salvatierra had gotten Kino's reports on the shells and the trek to the Colorado which was ample proof about a land passage. Since he was shipping cattle to California by sea at a cost of $300 a head, even the worst desert in the world would offer a cheaper overland route. Then, by late February both Salvatierra and Manje were rapping at the door of Kino's adobe in Dolores. It had been five years since the two priests were in Mexico together and ten since they rode through the Pimería discussing the future of the missions. Now they were teamed up for an historic journey west.

Before Padre Kino could safely leave Dolores, he had to fortify the mountain missions because the Apaches were opening a new and bold campaign of attack all around the Sierra Azul, the heartland of the Pimería. Salvatierra, on the other hand, knowing Piman fluently from his days as a missionary in Chínipas, went on ahead preaching his way through the valley of the Río Magdalena. A week later Kino caught up with the party at Caborca, and they set out for Sonoita where provisions were being assembled. This time, however, the explorers were determined to bypass the

1701

Gran Desierto

Devil's Highway and find a direct route to the mouth of the Colorado so certain were they that the Gulf terminated at this latitude.

What might have been one of the most significant expeditions of the careers of both Kino and Salvatierra was bungled by a half-wit Indian guide. Apparently that summer, trustworthy guides came at an unpayable premium; already some had refused to disclose watering places on the trail up from Caborca. Salvatierra wanted to go due west from Sonoita which would have brought them north of Pinacate into impassable sand dunes in the Gran Desierto. Kino listened to the Indian guides who favored a passage south of Pinacate. Manje argued for the only rational path – the Devil's Highway.

Kino prevailed. They turned south around Pinacate onto the horrifying volcanic mesa spewed out by the burned-out mountain. All Salvatierra could think of was what the world would look like after the final ordeal by fire. All they encountered – save for a few destitute Indians and a withered centenarian – were ashes, boulders, and sand. Water became a critical problem, particularly for the animals. The guides recommended a trail along the Gulf shore, so they inched across the searing boulders and sand. For three days they searched out a way; it was hopeless. The water at Tres Ojitos just north of modern Puerto Peñasco was insufficient and the remainder of the pack train they had left at the foot of Pinacate had to be brought back to water. Reluctantly they turned back. Once again, the desert sand would stall progress.

Having replenished their supplies at Sonoita, they set out again toward the north, but the Pima guides refused to enter into Yuman territory. It was a bad show all around. But the trio did manage to climb a steep, high peak north of Pinacate and from its heights they viewed a sunset glinting on the not so distant California mountains. Salvatierra was satisfied, but Kino and Manje were disgruntled. By violating their unwritten law of conquering the tierra incognita by known quantities, they lost the marvelous opportunity to link the Californias inseparably to the Pimería during their lifetimes. Realizing that neither time nor supply was on their side, the leaders returned to San Marcelo de Sonoita. Salvatierra, now even more anxious about California's survival hastened straight back to Cucurpe and to the Yaqui; he was back at Loreto in a month. Kino and Manje split off and returned via San Xavier del Bac because of their great concerns about peace in the Pimería – only to learn on arrival that the Pimas had struck a mighty blow against the Apaches who had been marauding in the region when the expedition was forming.

THE CROSSING OF THE COLORADO

Word spread through the Pimería of the new confirmations of Kino's discoveries. Another expedition was planned by the indefatigable trio for October. But Salvatierra had to beg off because Mission Loreto in California lacked horses to explore the west side of the Gulf. Manje unfortunately was caught in a reshuffling of assignments when a missionary in the mountains pleaded for a punitive force against hostile witch doctors. More ominous than anyone realized, however, was the replacement of General Jironza whose lifetime appointment over the Flying Company was dissolved in favor of General Jacinto Fuensaldaña, the military governor of the Province of Sinaloa. Surreptitiously the wily miner from Valladolid had purchased the title at the same time he falsely accused Jironza before the King. So Kino was left holding the reins of the expedition all alone, blissfully unaware of the social tempest the incoming commander would unleash across the Pimería. Don Jacinto was a past master at extortion and bribery.

Kino was now keenly anxious to reach the headlands of California that were known only to him through the long lens of his telescope. With the Pimería safe and secure, the crops harvested, and the round-up complete, he set out on November 3, 1701. Remaining resourceful as ever, he opened yet another new route westward across the Papaguería and along the Camino del Diablo to San Pedro on the Gila and San Dionisio at the junction of the rivers. Hundreds of Yumans and Pimans thronged around the Blackrobe just as they had done the year before. Kino was in his element, but as the cavalcade moved south along the Colorado, fear gripped one of the Spanish servants. A full quarter hour had elapsed before Padre Kino realized the poor Spaniard had ridden off in terror of his life. Two Pima cowhands chased after him on the fastest horses in the train, but they could not catch the timid, terrified man. No doubt he would hatch some choice rumors to exonerate his cowardice. Well, it wouldn't be the first time rumors reached the Pimería that Kino had been eaten alive by angry savages.

Padre Kino was touched in observing that the Yumas and the Quiquimas were fascinated by the celebration of the Mass. He was amused by their reaction to the horses and mules which they had never seen before. When the Quiquimas were told that horses could run faster than the Indians, they scoffed incredulously. So the Dolores cowboys arranged a race and the fleet footed Quiquimas dashed ahead of the ambling horses; then the spurs were put to their flanks and the galloping steeds passed the astonished natives in a victorious cloud of dust.

The horses may have been excellent for exploration, but they needed to have the brush cleared away in order to negotiate the river banks. It was obvious they couldn't swim the swift Colorado. Yet the Quiquimas insisted that Kino visit their lands on the opposite side. Nothing could be more agreeable because Kino was hoping to reach the shores of the great South Sea still ten days to the west.

Dry timbers were lashed together for a raft, and the horses were led toward the shaky craft; however, the horses mired down and shied from the strange surface of rippling timbers. Even Padre Kino was reluctant to get his boots wet — not because he was fastidious, but he knew well how essential good footgear is to the desert explorer. So the Indians fastened a large waterproof basket on the raft and Kino carefully sat down in his private compartment for the historic crossing of the Colorado.

His sojourn in Quiquima land was brief but hospitable. He knew he had to return to Dolores because the Spaniard who deserted him might cause untold troubles for the Indians of the west should the garrison at Real de San Juan or Fronteras mount a search for a "missing" Padre Kino. At least Kino was now absolutely sure the Gulf ended to the south of the juncture of the Gila and the Colorado and that a land route to Loreto was possible. Back on the east bank of the river the Padre was laden with two hundred loads of foodstuffs as gifts from the Quiquimas. What he gratefully accepted he graciously gave to the needy Yumas whose crops had failed that year.

The news of the crossing of the Colorado hardly jolted the Pimería, now accustomed to the rapid advances made by the aging Padre on horseback. Everyone realized the immense importance of a land route, but one suspects that the Indian raids along the whole northern perimeter were sapping the Spanish strength. Back in Dolores by December 8, Kino the cartographer redrew his famous *Paso por tierra* map of 1695. The lines of rivers and locations of towns and villages he put in place became one of the best known maps of northern New Spain and spread all over Europe after its initial printing.

TRAGEDY ON THE TRAIL

No one could break free for the next entrada of 1702 except for Kino's old Jesuit stalwart, Padre Manuel González, who had first introduced Kino to the Pimería. His health was not the best, but his spirit was lifted high by the reports of new peoples and new lands to the west. The cavalcade that formed at Dolores in early February was worthy of the two missionaries. One hundred and thirty horses and mules, laden with provisions, were the core. Kino would amplify that with some of the 1000 head of cattle at Síboda! The whole Spanish colony must have been dumbfounded to think that Padre Kino with one other priest-companion and a few cowhands could move herds of animals in perfect peace across the open desert when they couldn't keep a goat or a mine secure for a month.

Padre González was a perfect trail companion. Of Mexican birth and just as old as Kino, he was as warmly received as Kino and equally enthusiastic about the extensive mission foundations that could be set up on the Colorado. Crossing the Papaguería had become almost routine

1702

except for the fact that Kino was now increasing the number of ranches along the route to guarantee food and relays for the growing size of the expeditionary forces. Leap-frogging along the water tanks and holes of the Camino del Diablo, they reached the Yumas by March 1, 1702, Ash Wednesday. Little did either realize how much of a Lenten penance this journey would inflict! The pair directed the pack train south from San Dionisio and studied ways of crossing the immense river. The difficulties remained the same: the horses mired down and the rafts were useless. To complicate the problems, Padre González became very ill. Pain and hardship were constant companions to any missionary, so the discomfort Padre González experienced along the trail was in his mind nothing out of the ordinary. But the long hours in the saddle had aggravated an old hemorrhoid condition, and the rugged travel and exposure to winter weather was not helping at all.

Padre Kino now realized it would be impossible to cross the river and penetrate to the Pacific coast. No time could be lost in getting González back to help. The extreme urgency can be learned from the fact that Padre Kino turned due east from where he was on the Colorado! He committed himself to crossing the sand dunes of the Gran Desierto, the Sahara of Sonora. Howling winds lashed the company with stinging sand. The animals and men sank in the dry drifts making every step in advance an agony of frustration. They had fought their way nearly forty miles, about half-way to Pitaqui Peak, when they simply had to give up. They retraced their vanished steps and turned back along the more reliable river trails. Padre González braved his painful condition down the Devil's Highway, to him now so appropriately named. Reaching Sonoita, he rested for three days but his condition worsened. Loyal Pimas placed him on a litter and carried him on their shoulders across the desolate Papaguería. Already at the watering tank of Santa Sabina, Kino administered the last rites to the weak and nearly unconscious Blackrobe.

Padre Ignacio Iturmendi, the young missionary of Tubutama, met the desperate and now bedraggled cavalcade a few leagues outside of the village. Word had spread quickly of the expedition's predicament. González was lingering between life and beckoning death; nothing brought him relief or strength. Kino dispatched urgent pleas for medical assistance in the vain hope that someone's skills could alleviate Padre

San Pedro y San Pablo de Tubutama

Manuel's distress. It was not to be. In ten days he died.

Curiously enough those three Fathers who met under such trying circumstances would all be dead within ten years, and each would lie buried in the same chapel for centuries awaiting discovery and the honors of historical fame.

The death of Padre González was a blow, but the loss did not diminish the important findings of the expedition. A land passage to California was beyond a dream; it was hard truth, and proven. A mainland port on the Pacific could at last end the agony of anxiety which dogged the Manila galleon; it could mean naval supremacy for the whole hemispheric coast; it would halt the advance of Russia into the New World. And above all it would mean an earlier Christianization for the tens of thousands of Indians hunting and scrabbling out an existence in the chaparral of the Southwest.

Obviously, the loss of an experienced missionary like Padre Manuel on an expedition of exploration fanned the flames of criticism. Nor was the Pimería the same under the surly leadership of Fuensaldaña and his nephew Gregorio Tuñón y Quirós. Jironza had his critics and his supporters who were astonished at his sudden removal that had overtones

79

of expansionist politics. Who would ultimately control the fortunes to be ushered in by a villa on the Colorado? How could anyone allow this system to expand to the Colorado or beyond? How could anyone justify Kino's trips into the unknown interior? No wonder he had to spend so much time writing and arguing his case.

CONFINED TO QUARTERS

Not even Kino had solved the practical problem of crossing the mighty Colorado with its brushy banks, swirling currents, endless bogs, and twisting tributaries. Once again, Padre Eusebio set pen to paper and elicited support from every frontier figure upon whom he could rely – in this he missed González most. A brief trip down the Río Sonora to Guepac found him face to face with Father Visitor Leal, who, thank God, was still a believer in Kino's plan. But now Kino's relentless efforts to reach Alta California and the distant seas would have to subside long enough for him to dedicate his energy in revisiting the missions of the west and the north. What had plagued Kino most kept right on giving him trouble – the lack of priests in the missions. Indians now had come from all over the north and west begging for a resident priest. There were simply none to be assigned. Since this was a problem out of Kino's control, he did what he did best – he rode to the distant pueblos and engaged in the construction of churches, houses, and farms. He was building simultaneously at Sonoita, Búsanic, Sáric, and San Xavier del Bac – not to mention the large structure underway at Caborca. Without advertising it, Kino was laying a logistical foundation for the missionary conquest of California. Maybe there were no men to send, but when the time providentially would come, there would be facilities to meet all demands.

Kino's trip to Mexico in 1696 had released an avalanche of interest and support for the north. And now with the enthusiasm of his discovery of the land route to California, he knew no viceroy or provincial could refuse his requests. He appealed to Father Visitor Leal for permission to go to the capital once again. The trip could easily be made in the winter after the harvests were in and the round-ups complete. Leal was convinced. But others were not. Sonora was split into warring factions each of which included its share of Blackrobes and officials; Fuensaldaña himself was wary of how Kino's pleas might register with the Viceroy.

Word filtered back to Sonora that the time was inopportune because the new crop of missionaries had been detained in Cádiz by the suspension of the flota. No one was anxious to hear the ebullient Kino plead for more men and money; after all these were times to trim back, to conserve, to sit tight – all the kinds of things that clashed with Eusebio's natural disposition. But he learned to put up with the reversals by reason of his religious obedience. No men, no money still didn't mean no progress. He worked in earnest on two elegant churches close to Dolores – the twin churches of Cocóspera and Remedios. This was precisely the kind of endeavor that placated his critics because they feared him less with an ax and trowel in hand than a rein and an astrolabe. With California very much on his mind Kino had to cool his ardor for the rest of 1702. What had not been foreseen at the beginning of the spring expedition was the political effect of a cédula from Philip V, which was very positive about expansion but it called for detailed reports about the conditions of the missionary frontier. This was ample ammunition to hold Kino back and force him to dedicate his energies to more predictably pastoral activities.

Making almost weekly trips to Cocóspera and Remedios, Kino directed work on the domed churches that surpassed Dolores in design and elegance. Even in the building of the churches, Kino did not lose sight of his ambitious goals. Transept chapels in each were dedicated to St. Francis Xavier, the Apostle of the Indies. While construction pro-ceeded, bands of Indians from all over the Pimería streamed into Dolores to petition Fathers for their villages, as Kino had promised on his trips. But still there were no Fathers and Padre Eusebio had to console them with a few gifts, an occasional visit, and renewed promises. 1703 worked its way to a close. No expeditions had been organized. California was still inaccessible overland. And even as the churches neared completion, their dedications, originally scheduled for the feast of St. Francis Xavier, were postponed because of cantankerous litigation against the missions. For the whole year a lieutenant at San Juan Bautista (near Cumpas) was ac-cusing Pimas of all kinds of hostilities and robberies. He sent units into the western deserts to raid villages in punishment for their transgressions – which were all found to be trumped up. The lieutenant was summarily arrested and jailed for his treasonable conduct – and the Pimería settled back to a more peaceful routine.

1703

Litigation behind and ruffled feathers smoothed, the time had come to celebrate. Word spread through the desert villages of the great fiesta to be held at Cocóspera and Remedios. And in the midst of preparations, a new missionary appeared almost out of the blue. Padre Gerónimo Minutuli had lingered in the California missions which were struggling; he felt his presence would be more effective in the Pimería where he could help to stabilize the opening of the western trail to the coast. What a Christmas present for the Pimas who had been clamoring for assistance. Kino escorted his Italian companion to Tubutama, promising to build a new church on the spot. Kino was beaming, but the settlers in Sonora were furious to see the Jesuit plan of expansion continue to succeed.

SOARING DOMES AND CELEBRATIONS

The winter of 1704 was cold and rainy. But all who could responded to Kino's invitation to the dedications. Blackrobes, officers, Indian chiefs, and hordes of followers converged on Nuestra Señora de Remedios January 15 and 16. Padre Adam Gilg, now rector of the mission district of Dolores, sang the Mass; solemn blessings were pronounced; the Indians danced. The festivities warmed the chill winter air. Even if some Spaniards were skeptics, they had to admit the dozens of blue shells the natives had brought as gifts were stunning proof that the news of an overland route to the South Sea had to be true. Even more came to the dedication at Cocóspera on the 18th, 19th, and 20th – a true fiesta! Maybe those opposed to the missions had stalled Kino the explorer, but they couldn't stem the surge of native enthusiasm. They were living proof that there was a way west and a reason to go there. No small minded bureaucrat was going to dampen their desires for conversion and incorporation into the expanding empire.

Herbal Medicines at Magdalena

1704

One of the quieter participants at the dedication was Brother Juan Esteyneffer (Steinhoffer), an energetic Bohemian Jesuit. When Minutuli was setting out for Tubutama, Esteyneffer accompanied him and the other two German Province Jesuits, Kino and Gilg. It was a miniature example of what Kino had dreamed of years before in inviting members of the Germanic provinces to help in the evangelization of California and the Pimería. What makes Brother Juan's presence significant is that for several more years he roamed the desert missions teaching Indians the intricacies of herbal medicine, which survived into the 20th century so firmly in tact that some ethnographers thought the herbal medicine practiced in the desert was of native origin! One can only wonder at the immense influence these university trained Jesuits had on the transformation of native life.

But yet another serious problem was developing in the Pimería about this time. The military commander of the Flying Company for a short time had been General Jacinto Fuensaldaña. However, he became so embroiled in problems with the soldiers that the governor of Nueva Vizcaya intervened by ordering General Andrés Rezábel to arrest him because of alleged criminal conduct. Resourceful as always and aided by loyal advocates, he escaped to Mexico to assuage the Viceroy with glowing reports of adherents' support! It is no wonder that Kino speaks so constantly in his memoirs of the scandalous opposition he seems to have encountered forever and from all directions. Sonora's military fate was handed down to young Tuñón y Quirós – which left all the missions with next to no protection. It would be two more years before Fuensaldaña talked his way out of incarceration and back into his post as commander of Fronteras. Even then, returning in the heat of June he lasted only five months, dying in November, 1706. Once again the presidio reverted into the hands of Don Gregorio, the watchful nephew who had learned many of Jacinto's tricks. Nevertheless, Kino was kind to both, but how he would have much preferred to see the more experienced Juan Mateo take control of the fortunes of Sonora!

Clearly discord in Sonora among the Spanish settlers, the missionaries, and the military was taking its toll on the plan to support distant California. After the dedications of the churches were complete, Salvatierra wrote about the plight of the peninsular missions whose supplies had plunged to critical levels because they were used up in feeding the survivors of some ships wrecked on the California coast. Kino understood the problem well and decided to open a fast supply route over seldom traveled trails to the new harbor at Guaymas. Father Francisco María Piccolo was assigned there in order to build a staging station for maritime supply. It would be much closer to the opulent Sonora missions than the circuitous path along the Río Yaqui. So Kino was now determined to open the route via Opodepe and Pitic. With Easter festivities concluded, he set out March 25 for the gulf port; it took eight days to cross the sloping flatlands flanked by the Cerro Grande. At the time, Piccolo was away visiting the Yaqui missions, and rather uncharacteristically Kino refused an invitation to visit the Jesuits at those missions. Because Padre Eusebio was anxious to return to Dolores, Padre Francisco hastened to Guaymas to be with him for four days. The Indians were especially glad to see Kino because he was skilled in the Piman language and spent many hours instructing and encouraging them. So pleased was he with his trip, Padre Eusebio sent back a handsome gift to Piccolo, an oil painting of Señor San José in a gilt frame – what a treasure for the harbor mission of San José de Guaymas!

Nuestra Señora de la Asunción de Opodepe

Detouring through the Sonora River valley on his return from Guaymas, Kino learned of some major changes in government and the issuance of yet another royal cédula in favor of mission expansion. Among the communiqués from Mexico was a reconfirmation of Kino as rector of Dolores – an appointment that drew from him a burdensome sigh and an admission that bureaucratic overseeing was not to his liking, but he would discharge these responsibilities because it was God's will. Oh for the aches of riding horseback and not the strains of writing reports! 1704 bumbled along with no clear plans for an expedition and continuing hassles over calumnious accusations against the Pimas. Kino felt obliged to introduce the very Indians about whom vicious rumors were circulating to obstinate critics among the colonists. The Pimería could prosper in peace if these faint-hearted gossips could only be silenced. Maybe things might change because Padre Juan María had gone back to Mexico City – only to learn en route that the recently arrived Provincial and Visitor General Manuel Pineiro had died unexpectedly, naming unsuspecting Salvatierra as his successor! Padre Juan María like Eusebio was much more attracted to life on the frontier than behind a candle and quill. Yet, a friend like Salvatierra in such a high place might make a difference in assignments for the northwest. The change would come, but not for a whole year. Kino had to content himself with reading, writing, and managing his army of carpenters.

PLOTS AND PREPOSTEROUS ALLEGATIONS

Whatever the political factions were in Sonora, these were bad times for everyone. No sooner had Kino settled in at Dolores to reap the spring harvests and prepare for the summer heat than rumors flooded the region along with the seasonal storms. Some of Kino's most loyal Pima chiefs were being accused of plotting rebellion, including the murder of a missionary. Preposterous as it was, enough settlers believed the calumnies that fear gripped the mining camps. Once again, Kino rode out to the trouble spot, invited the Indians to accompany him, and returned to demonstrate to the Spaniards that the Pimas were not at war. And that was the way things went through Christmas, 1704. All was peace and joy.

That is, it was until shortly after the holidays. An unnamed and "indiscreet" lieutenant, who was obviously more strong willed than the

1705

interim captain of Fronteras, spread vicious lies about Kino's forcible gathering of Indians at his mission of Dolores. Just about everything had been tried to discredit Kino now for years; this was the first all-out attack on him personally – save for Padre Mora's diatribes eight years before. To save the Indians from their involuntary servitude the lieutenant sent a detachment to Dolores to seize over ninety Pimas who were exiled with high hopes that their relatives would turn on the beloved missionary. These were harsh times for Padre Eusebio. And the lieutenant knew how to hurt him. He took another detachment to punish some people living with Chief Coro, the unswerving loyal leader who was the bulwark against the Apaches. Coro advised him to take things easy, but the lieutenant instead denounced Coro as plotting a general uprising in the Pimería. Now the frontier was teetering on the brink of terror – too many consistent rumors were tumbling on top of one another. Tell enough lies and people begin to think it is the truth.

Not Kino. Quick to respond to the damaging gossip, he joined Coro and the other leaders and sent messages to places where troops might assemble. There was no cause for alarm. In a matter of weeks the trouble-making, would-be Spanish hero was sacked and the Pimería returned to a long deserved calm. It was already Easter time, so Kino leaned heavily on the splendor of religious ritual to reconcile all parties and rejoice in the return to a renewed life. And best of all, the Indians who had been forcibly removed from Dolores were restored to their chosen pueblos.

California and a New Missionary

California again dominated concerns in 1705. Father Piccolo had a chance to visit Dolores and the missions of the Pimería. There was ample talk of the supply of cattle and grains to be sent via the port of Guaymas. In fact, interest in the northwest missions had taken on new importance because Father Salvatierra, as Provincial, made a trip to the peninsula, marking the first time ever that such an eminent official had ever ventured so far afield. It bode well for Kino; he was at last officially recognized for what he had been doing for years – he was named Procurator of the northwest missions.

1705

The new responsibility was conferred on him by letter that came in mid-January, 1706. And more than that, the word came with the arrival of a new man for Caborca, Father Domingo Crescoli, a Napolitano with ten years experience in the Tarahumara. Losing no time to form an expedition westward, Kino brought him to Tubutama where they joined with Padre Gerónimo Minutuli; the three Italians headed southwest: Crescoli to Caborca, Kino and Minutuli to explore the Gulf coast. Although Kino's memoirs are jumbled in the dates, the party spied the great island of Tiburón, which they named Santa Iñes in honor of her feast on January 21. It had been almost twenty years since Padre Eusebio had summered on the south side of the bay that now bears his name; the northern shore where they encamped, they called Cabo San Vicente, now Desemboque. Like all dedicated travelers of the Sonoran desert, the two could not resist the splendor of the spring with vast fields of grass and wild flowers. Having been sensitized to herbal medicines by Brother Esteyneffer, Kino was quick to note the proliferation of jojoba that was in demand all over New Spain. But it was time to turn back. The spring meant planting and planning. As they passed through Caborca, Padre Domingo greeted them joyfully. Shortly afterwards, however, he slips from the record of the Piman missions; his health was too delicate for the scorching lowland desert.

Lent began early in 1706, so Padre Kino took advantage of the season to make an extended trip to the northwest to teach, preach, and administer ashes to the clusters of Christian Indians that were now springing up all over the desert. But there was a new tone to his travels, he learned to appease his critics by emphasizing the discharge of his pastoral duties and not the prowess of his scientific mind. Like so many things in life when less energetic people begin to criticize, it was presumed that if Kino were making such extensive forays into unknown territory that he simply had no time left to evangelize. But the evidence to the contrary was overwhelming because hundreds of Indians tramped over leagues of desert to appeal for a missionary to live among them – someone like Kino they hoped!

Cresoli's departure from Caborca placed another great burden on Padre Eusebio because the westernmost mission was on the verge of harvesting good winter wheat and the church buildings were rising fast. With his army of carpenters and skilled laborers, he worked on building at Tubutama, Caborca and Búsanic. Ever since Salvatierra sat in the

Provincial's seat in Mexico, there had been talk of new missionaries for the Pimería. Weekly it seemed a mysterious four-man team was to appear to take over at Caborca, San Cayetano (Tumacácori), Santa María Suamca, and San Xavier del Bac. They never came, yet preparations continued as if they would. Most of 1706 was thus consumed with hard work and expectations. And Kino's enthusiastic appraisal of the "short" route to California via the island of Santa Iñez triggered the ambitions of Padre Juan de Ugarte who began to solicit funds for a vessel to carry the supplies. Kino answered his suggestions, however, by telling him that they did not need to buy a boat because he had continued to work on gathering the materials for one already. But despite the time, the labor, and the renewed momentum, the craft was never completed – leaving the door wide open for Ugarte eventually to build his own famous *Triunfo de la Santa Cruz* fourteen years later.

DISCOVERIES VERIFIED

Making a short trip to Fronteras in September to acquire clothing for his mission wards, Padre Kino had a chance to discuss his plans for expansion with General Fuensaldaña back in command after his Mexico interlude. The chief military officer agreed completely with Kino and pledged his support for another expedition to verify the validity of a land passage to California. Padre Eusebio was elated because the Quiquimas of the Río Colorado had been coming to Tubutama with gifts of shells and curious gaming balls from the coastal tribes. With the general's backing, Kino organized an expedition by October. In contrast to recent trips, this one would have a full military escort and the presence of a Franciscan.

Sierra Santa Clara (Pinacate Peak)

Fray Manuel de Oyuelas, from Guadalajara. If the skeptics and naysayers wouldn't believe Kino after all these years, they would have to listen to these trail companions. The route

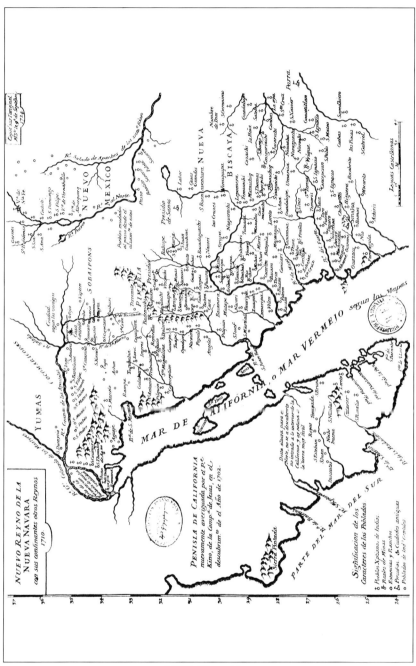

1710 Kino Map

was the familiar one from Dolores to Tubutama, Caborca and Sonoita. In his own account of the journey, Oyuela was impressed with the preaching and teaching ability of the wizened Blackrobe. At sixty-two Kino still had the stamina to talk long into the night. Having reached Sonoita, Kino decided not to make the arduous ride over the Camino del Diablo, but to strike out for the Sierra Santa Clara from whose heights his fellow travelers could see the head of the Gulf and the mountains of the California peninsula. Both Alférez Juan Mateo Ramírez and Antonio Durán, the military officers, and Fray Oyuela were genuinely convinced as eye witnesses of what Kino had discovered now years ago. With all this evidence, corroborated by agents of Fuensaldaña, Mexico and Madrid would have to listen! Yet, as fate would have it, just as the certifications were being signed at Dolores in late November, word came that General Jacinto had died! Could there be any more surprises or set-backs?

Twenty years had now elapsed since Kino first clattered into Cosari, the Piman village that became the mission headquarters of Dolores, Our Lady of Sorrows. Surrounded by prospering missions and ranches, plagued with a lack of missionary auxiliaries, and frustrated in reaching California by land, Kino's last years were a marvel of resilience. The opposition which he constantly alludes to in his memoirs was reaching a crescendo because the sheer prosperity of the missions in the Pimería was over-powering the puny efforts of Spanish settlers and ex-soldiers. Those who had dedicated their lives to becoming rich miners were still blocked by Kino's staunch application of the King's cédula that had excused Indian converts from labor in the mines for twenty years – but those years were nearly over. The Pimería of 1707 was a different land standing in the midst of changed circumstances. All the infighting Kino had experienced over the last several years could be reduced to the perennial impasse over colonialism – it was exploitation versus protection. And right in the middle were the Indians and their resources.

The once young and vibrant Manje had prospered as a miner and rancher, but he, too, was feeling the press of mission dominance. No sooner had Fuensaldaña died than Manje enlisted the support of fellow Sonorans to protest the power of the Jesuits and the plight of the colonists by taking the case to the Viceroy, the Duque de Albuquerque. Piccolo, still the Father Visitor for the northwest, exploded and put pressure on

1707

Juan Fernández de Córdoba, Governor of Nueva Vizcaya.

While Kino watched in dismay, the rancorous Manje was summarily arrested and jailed in distant Parral where he wrote scathing couplets against the Sonoran Jesuits – but not Kino whose sense of fairness was known to all. Manje's *cause célebre* soon embroiled the Audiencia in Guadalajara and the Bishop of Durango who was secretly advocating the secularization of all the Jesuit missions! Then, realizing that the issue might jeopardize everyone's interests, the Jesuits interceded with Córdoba to ease up on Manje while all parties searched for a compromise. And really no solutions were found because the Jesuits could not find new missionaries; the Bishop could find no seculars; and the miners had to respect the freedom of the Indians.

TURBULENCE, THEN PEACE

These turbulent events deeply affected Padre Eusebio. His informative *Favores Celestiales*, the memoirs of his labors in the Pimería Alta, in the last chapters reflect a jumble of events and a judicious editing of the last years. He specifically omits 1707, 1708, and 1709 with the summary statement that nothing really happened save the continuing arguments over expansion and the lack of adequate missionary support. How this intensely apostolic man absorbed the blows of criticism and overcame the disappointments of constant opposition confounds one's comprehension. Calmly, Kino closed the record of his last years by revising and substituting an old report he compiled for the King in response to his cédula of 1701. His last great literary effort was a compelling plea for more missionaries for the thousands of abandoned souls in northwest New Spain. No one listened. No one came.

Padre Agustín de Campos had been Kino's companion on the Pima frontier for eighteen years. He followed suit in building up his mission and visitas. In fact, since the dedication of Remedios and Cocóspera he worked hard on his churches along the Río Magdalena. Kino spoke with praise for the fine church Campos was building at Santa María Magdalena; it was only a few miles south of San Ignacio and nestled in a fertile valley that opened onto the sprawling desert toward the west. It was very close to Tupo where peace had been made with the Pima chieftains after the martyrdom of Saeta. In 1711, Kino still continued his strong devotion to St. Francis Xavier, whom he always considered the saint who had interceded for his life. With the Novena of Grace just terminated, there was an excellent opportunity to dedicate the newly completed chapel in Xavier's honor. It was twenty-four years, almost to the day, when Padre Eusebio had first entered the Pimería and ridden into the Magdalena valley. What a marvelous occasion to celebrate! With Campos in attendance, he began the Mass of dedication. But something suddenly overcame the trail-hardened missionary. He felt abnormally weak. Campos assisted him from the chapel to a small room where Kino lay down on his saddle blankets. This would be his last ride, for the Blackrobe slipped away about midnight, March 15, 1711. His earthly explorations were done; his heavenly ones, just begun.

Even incomplete records of his expeditions give a total of over eight thousand miles on horseback through the most hostile desert on the continent. A day's ride continued to average well over thirty miles, not accounting for side trips to visit the sick, to instruct and baptize. With him he drove herds of cattle, sheep, goats, horses, and burros. How these animals were fed and watered was a problem that apparently only the genius of Kino could resolve.

Padre Kino had lingered on the brink of discovery throughout most of his life. He had sailed the Atlantic, studied the stars, crossed the Colorado, charted the approaches to the California coast, crisscrossed the head of the Gulf, crossed the Colorado, and defied the Gran Desierto itself. While he was unraveling rumor from fact in the western haze, a mission frontier behind him struggled to keep pace. He had led armies of carpenters, bricklayers, farmers, and irrigation experts in the build-

Kino's remains *in situ* at Magdalena

ing of a frontier that would succor distant California.

His life was over, but a dream was coming true. Padre Kino had come to a desert. He came among abandoned peoples. He rode the arid trails. He bore the acid criticism of colonials. Why? Because he recognized that the paradox of Christianity is locked in the paradox of the desert. Life is more precious where life seems unable to survive. People are dearer where people seem almost out of place. Peace is more possible where man recognizes the potentials of hostility.

The Pimería Alta had responded to the vision of Padre Eusebio. His dedication, his dreams, and his devotion had not changed the Pimería as much as it had brought it to life. But Padre Kino, like every man, had to come to the end of the trail...

Padre Campos chose the chapel of St. Francis Xavier for his burial place. And through the centuries since his death the village of Magdalena has been the focal point of an undiminished devotion to St. Francis Xavier. For dozens of decades the faithful from Sonora, Arizona, Chihuahua, Sinaloa, and California have traveled hundreds of miles, many of them on foot, to

Kino's crypt in Magdalena

participate in the fiesta of San Francisco. The reason baffles many people. But ethnologists offer a simple explanation: the Indians have simply transformed Padre Kino's devotion to San Francisco into one of mutual homage to the patron of the Pimería and to the pioneer padre himself. And who knows but what they're right?

Nuestra Señora del Pilar y Santiago de Cocóspera

THE PIMERÍA ALTA
BEFORE AND AFTER PADRE KINO

Padre Kino looms as a lonely giant on the unknown horizons of southwestern history. But this is more an illusion created by a climate of ignorance than by an intentional distortion of historiography. Kino did not labor alone, nor were his accomplishments significant because of their singularity. Padre Kino was only one of many who devoted life and talent so that the Pimería might take its rightful place among nations. Kino's exploits gained prominence not because they were performed in a remote and isolated land, but because they were the deeds of a most extraordinary man among extraordinary men. It would be unfair, an inaccuracy of history, to omit mention of others who worked before, with, and after Kino on this frontier. They shared at least a part of his vision, and they mutually shaped the fortunes of this land.

Jesuit mission expansion in northwestern New Spain had been rapid and successful. In 1591 two Blackrobes began work at the Villa of San Felipe near Culiacán, Sinaloa, and in less than a decade the mission frontier leaped northward from the river deltas into the mountain fastnesses of the Sierra Madre Occidental. Working systematically with an increasing number of men, the Jesuits reached the Río Yaqui in southern Sonora by 1617. In that quarter century the mission field had expanded from two priests serving hundreds in Sinaloa to more than thirty men ministering to thousands along the whole northwest coast.

1591

1617

Contact with the native peoples of central Sonora was made in 1621, but the momentum of mission expansion slowed considerably after 1626 when the great frontier captain Don Diego

1621

1626

Christopher Corbally, S.J. at Cucurpe Ruins

Martínez de Hurdaide retired from service. Civil and military affairs were entrusted to Don Pedro de Perea, who had distinctly different ideas about frontier expansion and exploitation. Perea soon settled on a plan to carve out a new kingdom, Nueva Andalucía, over which he would rule. His personal attention focused on the remote valley of the Río Sonora, above the great bend near Ures. This lush, desert valley was ideal for farming and ranching; the flanking hills cloaked rich veins of silver and gold. Perea chose the valley as the site of his hacienda and brought his wife, Doña María Ibarra, to Banámichi. Fearing the influence of the Jesuit missionaries over the Indian populace of the valley, Don Pedro invited five Franciscans from New Mexico into central Sonora. Already claiming the establishment of several missions throughout the area, the Jesuits confronted Perea and challenged his intentions.

1645

In 1645 Perea determined to send the grayrobed friars of St. Francis into the unevangelized territory of the Hymeris, as the Pimas Altas were then known. An expedition was prepared to enter the land from Cucurpe, but Perea was taken violently ill on July 31, the feast of St. Ignatius. He reluctantly returned to Tuape. In a few weeks he recovered and set out with the same goal, but this time, taking sick again, he died on October 4, the feast of St. Francis Assisi! It would almost seem that the founders of the two orders were involved in this Sonoran rivalry.

1650

Perea's death plunged the province into turmoil. The Jesuits urged their exclusive claim to operate missions throughout Sonora, and the Franciscans acquiesced by agreeing to leave Sonora in 1650. Immediately the Jesuits prepared to move deep into the Pimería Alta; Padres Pedro Bueno and Francisco París were selected as emissaries to the new conversions among the Pimas. But just as their cavalcade started into the territory, the new military commander at the Real of San Juan Bautista, Don Juan de Peralta, ordered the entry to be stopped. Officially the Jesuits lost the much awaited chance to open new missions among the Pimas, but quite miraculously the pack animals of the cavalcade wandered throughout the Pimería and returned unscathed! Officialdom may have hardened the "Rim of Christendom" for a few years, but the burros of the Blackrobes had a good glimpse of a mission field that would have to wait for the coming of Padre Kino thirty-seven years later.

MARRAS: MISSIONARY EXTRAORDINAIRE

With the passing of Perea new policies and directions came to Sonora. Prospectors filtered into the harsh canyons searching for rich pockets of precious metals. Like most soldiers of fortune these *gambusinos* had little time left to care for themselves so they acquired food, clothing, and supplies on whatever credit might be extended. At this time in Sonoran

Church and bells at Tecoripa

history a remarkable Jesuit from Sardinia, Padre Daniel Angelo Marras, was assigned to San José de Mátape, the mission at the end of the Camino Real. Marras arrived just soon enough to learn the fine points of the Nebome language from Padre Lorenzo Cárdenas, the organizer of the upper Sonoran missions. Cárdenas died in 1656, leaving Mátape in the care of the young, enterprising Marras. His Indian mission was in the heart of the silver country, and it was to him the gambusinos came to beg supplies.

1656

If any single missionary changed the face of Sonora, it was Padre Daniel. Coming into a newly organized frontier, he recognized the critical position of the native communities. Quickly he won the admiration of the people and transformed the new missions into productive, agricultural centers. He begged and bartered for 600 head of breeding stock from the lower Sinaloa missions. By the time of Marras' reassignment to Puebla in 1681, he had increased the herd to over 50,000 head!

1681

The ranches under Marras' administration were so productive that cattle drives were initiated from Sonora to Mexico City in the 1680's. The industry that later became a distinguishing mark of Sonora was actually the stepchild of Padre Daniel, yet almost no one remembers or even knows of him. Agricultural production increased so much that Spanish farmers in the region accused him of overproduction and undercutting their inflated markets. And the wandering prospectors became so indebted that one man was obliged to sign over his properties to Mátape; in this curious manner Marras was plunged into the tumultuous business of mining and refining silver. Although critics have accused the missionaries of engaging in mining, which was strictly forbidden by the rules of the religious orders, Marras actually accepted mining claims in payment for debts owed to the *college* of Mátape, not the mission. These acquisitions were completely permissible because colleges did not fall under the same strictures as missions. Nonetheless, historical vagueness has confused the affair with the missions emerging as the losers. Subsequent rectors of the college of Mátape were ordered to sell the properties, which took several years to accomplish because the region remained so economically depressed; no one was able to buy. The cunning Sardinian of Sonora had witnessed some of Sonora's most prosperous days.

Only five years after Marras' departure, Padre Kino arrived in the Pimería Alta to take advantage of the fertile land and industrious natives. Essentially Kino did exactly as Marras had done – he also begged breeding stock and increased them into the tens of thousands. Most of the Sonoran missionaries benefited from the solid foundations Marras laid down, although few were as successful as Marras or Kino in the north. Padre Adam Gilg struggled to convert the simple, nomadic Seris, but neither land nor people were suited to industrious expansion. Padre Marcos de Loyola at San Ignacio de Cuquiarachi held the precarious line between Opatas and Apaches; his situation offered little hope for new conversions. To the north and west Padre Kino found inviting opportunities; he met the challenge with imagination and determination.

THE LONG REIGN OF AGUSTÍN DE CAMPOS

Kino shared the Pimería Alta with several missionaries. Probably the foremost among them was Padre Agustín de Campos who arrived in the early years of its development. In 1693, just after taking his final vows in the Society, Campos was assigned to San Ignacio de Caborica, near Magdalena. While Kino pushed farther toward the western reaches of the desert, Padre Agustín tended the missions of the heartland along the Magdalena and Santa María rivers. Quiet and stoic, Campos has

1693

received little recognition from history. Yet his journeys probably gave many Arizona sites their place names. Even Tucson preserves the patronage of St. Augustine and the Catalina Mountains, the faint memory of a Mass he once celebrated in a Piman village at their foot. Although Kino has been remembered for his extensive explorations, Campos rode the limits of the same frontier and penetrated the White Mountains in search of the Moqui. Kino spent twenty-four years putting the Pimería on the map; Campos spent forty-three years keeping it there. He frequently performed duty as chaplain to the hard-riding Flying Company of Sonora. Weeks on the trail made him a fast friend of Captain Juan Bautista de Anza, father of the colonizer of San Francisco. His last days were spent in the quiet of the Anza home at Fronteras, until he went reluctantly to Chihuahua where he died in 1737.

The first decade after Kino's death was difficult for the Pimería Alta. Manpower continued to be scarce, and the apostolic commitments did not dwindle. Kino's old mission of Dolores struggled to maintain its centrality; Father Luis Velarde, who was assigned there in 1714, had all _1714_ he could do to minister it together with Remedios and Cocóspera. Many have looked upon him as a successor to Kino, but he never distinguished himself as the explorer and traveler Kino was. However, he faithfully worked there until his death in 1737, a year in which the Pimería would lose many of its old guard. The recently established Christian communi- _1737_ ties in old Indian pueblos deserved at least an occasional visit from a missionary. San Xavier del Bac, Tubutama, Santa María Suamca, and Caborca had received constant attention from Kino. Caborca remained vacant after Padre Domingo Crescoli left in poor health. And Tubutama enjoyed the ministration of Padre Geronimo Minutuli, who often rode with Kino; but apparently Minutuli also left shortly after the death of Padre Kino – at least in 1712 Campos removed the remains of two Jesuits buried at Tubutama, which indicated the mission was probably vacant.

Nearly a decade passed after Kino's death before help arrived for the western missions. Once again Caborca received a Sicilian, Father Luis Gallardi, and similarly Tubutama received Father Luis Marziani. The Jesuits had no intention of abandoning those strategically important missions on the road to California. A change of policy was breathing new life into the beleaguered frontier. Since 1707, when the Jesuit administration was dominated by short-sighted perfectionists, the missions and the Indian neophytes suffered terribly; even the last years of Kino's life felt the harshness of restrictions that banned his explorations and expansion.

The coming of these two priests brought hope to those who still saw the Pimería as a land of promise. Velarde, although in poor health, was articulate in making appeals and stated the case well for expansion. Campos pleaded to the Viceroy in 1723 for a resurgence of royal support, resurrecting Kino's notion of a villa on the Colorado, although Campos apparently wanted to champion a maritime passage to upper California. Evidently he had been influenced by a brief meeting on the Gulf shores of Sonora in 1721 when Father Juan Ugarte was exploring the northern waters. Campos' geography was faulty, but his politics were on target. Impressed with the missionary's appeal, the Viceroy contacted Benito Crespo, Bishop of Durango, who made a lengthy tour of inspection of the northern tier of missions in his diocese in 1727. He urged the Crown to solicit more missionaries to serve the growing Christian communities. This was a curious turn in the wars of expansion and survival. King Felipe V responded to Crespo's suggestions by ordering the Viceroy to support new efforts in the Pimería Alta.

Guevavi Ruin

GERMAN REINFORCEMENTS

Results were not long in coming by colonial standards. 1730 brought the first new wave of missionaries to break over the desert lands. Some of them showed a vitality and optimism reminiscent of Padre Kino himself. The first of the new group was Father Gaspar Stiger, a Swiss from Oberried (St. Gallen), who came to San Ignacio in 1731 where he was tutored in the Pima dialects by the accomplished Father Campos. And when Campos relinquished his post in 1736, after forty-three years of service, Stiger took charge of San Ignacio, remaining there until his

1723

1727

1730

1731

death in 1762. While Padre Stiger studied the Piman languages at San Ignacio, another Swiss and two German missionaries arrived for assignment to long vacant missions. 1736

Strategically located, the mission of Santa María de los Pimas (Suamca) became the base of operations for Father Ignacio Keller. A gruff Moravian, he shortly undertook expeditions down the San Pedro, hoping like Campos, to link up with the Moqui (Hopi) villages of the north. On one hapless trip Keller and his Piman escorts were stripped of all their horses and supplies after they crossed the Gila into Apache country. Sheer stamina and courage protected them from total annihilation. As Keller approached a quarter century of service he found himself in the middle of a bitter controversy in which he was accused of triggering the bloody Pima rebellion of 1751, a story that will be told below. 1751

The other Swiss missionary to join in the revitalized efforts in the Pimería Alta was Father Philip Segesser, a nobleman of Lucerne. He was assigned to San Xavier del Bac, the largest Piman settlement in the region and also the most distant from the Spanish perimeter of defense. Since Kino founded the mission in 1700, permanent residency here had been nearly impossible. Segesser himself spent only a little more than a year in this fertile mission before he was recalled to Los Santos Angeles de Guevavi where Father Johann Grazhofer had died under mysterious circumstances (1733). Some years after Grazhofer's death an old Indian resident of Guevavi claimed that he had poisoned the missionary, but there is strong reason to doubt this since Grazhofer had been seriously ill with a fever he contracted on his way to the Pimería Alta. Remaining at Guevavi for about a year, Segesser then left for work in the missions of central Sonora.

Vacant for several years after the death of Father Ignacio Iturmendi and the departure of Gerónimo Minutuli, the mission of Tubutama reestablished its importance as a strategic center in the evangelization of the western deserts in 1721 with the coming of Father Luis Marciano. Hardly had Marciano gone to Tubutama than Campos journeyed to Mexico City, leaving San Ignacio in charge of the relatively young Sicilian. These were very unstable years for the Pima Alta missions. When Campos returned in 1723, Marciano opted for transfer to the central Sonora missions. And once again the stalwart Campos held the Pimería in his able

hands. As for Tubutama, it would remain a visita until 1736 when Father Jacob Sedelmayr, took charge. From the moment of his arrival, he watched great transformations take place in the frontier apostolate. Campos had been removed from San Ignacio; Gallardi, who comforted Campos at the time of his reassignment, died after just sixteen years of work at Caborca; Tubutama; San Xavier del Bac and Guevavi were still vacant. And Padre Sedelmayr was left alone at a post that demanded a vigorous missionary.

COURAGEOUS EXPLORATION

Sedelmayr of Bavaria was cut from the same cloth as Kino. He travelled extensively and looked on the Pimería with a progressive optimism that had been missing among the missionaries for many years.

102

Once again pack trains moved with regularity across the Papaguería to the villages on the Colorado. Exploring upward on the wide, red river, Sedelmayr reached the edges of Moqui country. Analysis of his travel diaries seems to indicate that he reached the Bill Williams River which he followed into central Arizona. The entradas of this blond-haired German were part of a concerted Jesuit effort to establish missions along the Gila and Colorado; the dream continued of building a Spanish villa at the confluence of those two historic rivers. But it was not to happen in Jesuit times, and when it did, the results were catastrophic because the Yuma Rebellion of 1781 effectively cut overland travel to the Pacific for nearly a half-century. By 1740 the official attitude on mission expansion was changing dramatically, but the quarter-century slow-down was difficult to overcome. Just as new speculations emerged, the Yaquis of lower Sonora conducted a most troublesome revolt that deeply affected the politics of leadership in the province. No sooner than the revolt was put down, the disastrous Pima rebellion of 1751 shattered a half-century of peace, one crafted and cherished by Kino himself.

The Pimería had been remarkably peaceful for three generations with the exception of the limited uprising in 1695. The climate for rebellion was probably created in the tumultuous 1730s when the Pimería Alta once again came to life under the ambitious Alcalde Mayor, Baron Gabriel Prudhón de Beltran Heider y Mujica. During his administration emphasis on exploiting the mineral wealth of the province attracted adventurers and soldiers of fortune to the desert frontiers. In 1736 a Yaqui Indian, Antonio Sirumea, stumbled onto a massive concentration of "virgin" silver in an arroyo west of the Cibuta Valley near a Piman settlement named Arizonac. Once word of

Diorama of Pima Revolt at Tumacácori

the discovery reached the interior of Sonora hundreds of hopeful colonials converged on the arid region. Some were fortunate enough to find large slabs of silver – one weighing as much as 2,500 pounds! Appalled by the discovery, the Jesuit missionaries could only see this as the occasion for an invasion by "the dregs of humanity" into mission lands. A strong case was made that the silver was not virgin, but that it had indeed been mined earlier by Spaniards or even Aztecs on their way to Mexico! The Jesuits insisted that the discovery was actually a treasure; in this way the law would deliver the silver to the Crown and block the immigration of opportunistic colonials. Bitter experience for a century and a half showed that Indian unrest soon followed the intrusive presence of mining camps.

REBELLION ON THE FRONTIER

Jesuit fears were not exaggerated because within fifteen years the unruly mining camps had introduced envy, hatred, ambition and anarchy into the Indian pueblos. Despite vehement protests by the missionaries, the Spanish governor for Sonora appointed a haughty Pima, Luis Oacpicagigua (Luis of Saric), as the responsible Indian governor of the Pimas Altos. Luis had served with presidial forces in campaigns against the Seris on the Gulf coast. He knew the strengths and weaknesses of the Spanish military. Within months of his appointment as Indian governor he organized a coordinated uprising of Pimas against the Spanish reales (mining towns) and missions. Scores of Spaniards were slaughtered and the missions put under siege. Padre Sedelmayr at Tubu-

Asumpción de Arispe

tama was wounded by a poisoned arrow, but recovered and escaped to the south. Not so, young Father Tomás Tello who was cut down at Caborca and Father Henrique Ruhen who was martyred on a desert trail near his mission of Sonoita. Before the Spaniards could react the whole of the Pimería was pillaged and left smoldering in ruin.

The rebellion itself was put down in a relatively short time, four months, but its effects rippled through the ensuing decade. In one sense its effects reached permanently into the future because Spanish frontier policy shifted in favor of a strong military presence. Presidios were stationed at Altar and Tubac, the latter being the place where the rebellion flared on a cold November morning in 1751. The small garrisons were designed to keep the Pimas in line, but the unrest and injustices that had triggered the rebellion also broke the loose tribal alliances among the Pimans themselves. With this disintegration the Spanish first line of defense against the Apache crumbled, and it was only a matter of time before the nomadic marauders had pushed deep into Sonoran territory, making pacts with Seris and Tepocas.

Under cover of Spanish cavalry the missionaries returned to their demolished churches to rebuild and start anew. Even though the frontier remained unsettled, a large new church was begun at San Xavier del Bac. In 1756 the new Governor of Sonora, Don Juan Antonio de Mendoza, laid the first adobe in place for the mission church. (Two hundred and ten years later archaeologists found its forgotten foundations just a hundred feet west of the imposing baroque successor). A new roster of missionaries filtered into the vacancies along the frontier as an optimistic future dawned once again for the Pimería. Explorations in the next decade were less bold because the rebellion had taught unfriendly Indians to be more brash. Nevertheless the Blackrobes rode to the distant Colorado and all along the Gila to visit the Christian communities that still remained faithful.

Twenty-two missions far to the south in Sinaloa and Durango were turned over to the Bishop as part of a plan of secularization. The transfer of responsibility released several Jesuits for new missions planned in Alta California, but the plans remained just that, plans. The Bourbon monarch, Charles III, extended his power through policies of militarization. Where frontier concerns had once focused on native pacification, the frontier was now regarded as a bulwark of defense in an international struggle for the acquisition and retention of land. The rancor between expansionists and missionaries that had bothered Padre Kino still infected the scene at mid-century. Expansion was a chameleon word. For the Crown it indicated the growing power of empire; for missionaries it meant the extension of protection for native peoples as a part of the process of conversion. To colonials on the frontier mission expansion was anathema because they felt the best lands should be theirs and that native peoples should become the labor pool in their bid for wealth. However one interprets the times, the future looked ominous for the Jesuits.

WORLD WIDE EXPULSION

1767

In 1767 the entire Jesuit missionary program, world-wide, was snapped like a brittle branch from the dying tree of the Spanish empire. By order of Charles III, the less than enlightened monarch of all the Spains, every Jesuit throughout the Spanish empire, more than 5,000 in all, was banished. With lightning swiftness each Jesuit missionary, teacher, and public servant was arrested and bound over to regional authorities for exile to Spain and other European countries. Jesuits born in the Americas were exiled from

San José de Guaymas

their homelands and scattered about in foreign countries. In many ways the expulsion of the Society of Jesus from Portugal, France, and, finally, Spain, and the Society's eventual suppression in 1773, were among the more curious events of the eighteenth century.

1773

No area under Spanish control was exempt from the King's decree which was executed in every case by the highest officials of the empire under the unusual penalty of death for failure to comply. The Pimería

Alta, like Patagonia and the Philippines, fell under the pall of Bourbon intrigue. In Sonora the Jesuits were arrested without previous warning and escorted in chains to the dilapidated college at Mátape in the south central part of the province. In the steamy heat of July, fifty-one former missionaries were gathered in the chapel where the decree of banishment was read; under cautious military guard the Blackrobes were marched down the sandy river trails to the seaport of Guaymas where they rendezvoused with other exiles on September 2. The all provident government would transport the exiles from there to San Blas, the Matanchel of Kino days. Except there was no ship!

By early August the embargo that Visitador General José de Gálvez had placed on the West coast of New Spain had taken full effect. No ship could be found to transport the Jesuits. Fishing boats and pearl divers were forbidden to put to sea. So the Blackrobes were confined to a provisional military compound hastily constructed for troops anticipated for General Domingo Elizondo's Seri campaign. The tiny barracks became home for clumps of missionaries, eight or nine crowded in dirt-floored rooms with leaky thatch roofs. For nine months the men remained under continual surveillance, without privacy for the most basic human needs. By May, 1768, the men were deathly sick, but relief came when a small French packet-boat, *El Príncipe*, arrived to take them into exile. Only fifty embarked; Padre José Palomino, a veteran of thirty-seven years in Sinaloa died in late November. The exiles' release from confinement was short lived, however, because spring storms clutched the sailing vessel and blew it across the Gulf to Puerto Escondido, just south of Loreto. There the dying Jesuits were confined to the now becalmed ship because Spanish officials feared reprisals from Visitor General Gálvez if they were allowed ashore. Finally at the insistence of Fray Junípero Serra, the newly installed Franciscan superior of the California missions, Governor Gaspar de Portolá broke down and permitted them to be brought ashore for rest and better care. For two weeks the Jesuits continued to improve, but as soon as news arrived that Gálvez was only a two day march away, the still sickly refugees were forced back on the ship which sailed immediately. Landing at San Blas, the once vigorous missionaries dropped in death as their forced march carried them from the tropical coast to the highlands of Guadalajara.

Twenty died under the extreme exertion-including Juan Nentwig of Guásavas, Manuel Aguirre of Bacadeguachi, and Pedro Díez of Atil; the majority were buried in the church of Ixtlan where death kindly absolved them from their torments. It pleased the Viceroy, the Marqués de Croix, to hear that almost half had died; the Crown would save so much money – but he hadn't calculated the 16,063 pesos in burial costs!

Had the officials of Guadalajara not intervened to stop the brutal mistreatment of the Sonoran Jesuits, the toll would have been appreciably higher. But their plight was immediately recognized by those who did not share the enlightened philosophy of the Bourbons. Fortunately, José de Gálvez, the Marqués de Sonora, was still far away in California and could not intervene. He would pose no threat to the powerful members of the Audiencia if they should order carriages for the weakened survivors and a medical doctor for the dangerously ill. The exiles' trip continued through Mexico City to Vera Cruz where the *Princesa Ulrica* took on the first nineteen survivors. Embarking in November, they did not land in Spain until April 26, 1769. Their tortuous ordeal had lasted nearly two years!

1769

Reaching Europe was no return to Paradise. The exiled Jesuits, if from foreign nations, were interrogated and sent back to their home countries. In many cases a lack of funds or the conditions of a prevailing war prevented repatriation. The royal answer to the dilemma of the unwelcome Jesuits was imprisonment on the second floor of the former Jesuit missionary hostel at Puerto Santa María across the bay from Cádiz. Several were never allowed out of confinement for as much as eight years! Eventually the last Jesuits were banished from Spain; most of the homeless sought refuge in Bologna, northern Italy. The great majority of them died there and were buried in a potter's field – including the famous Mexican historian Francisco Javier Clavijero.

THE END OF AN ERA

The expulsion of the Society of Jesus drew the curtain on the drama of Jesuit missionary activity in northwestern New Spain. It left the whole of the country without the skills of the Society's teachers, scientists, missionaries, and explorers. Valiantly the Franciscans tried to fill the vacuum left in the Pimería and in California. But the dispersal of the friars only thinned the ranks of already overworked missionaries. It was a task beyond the resources of the church of New Spain. A score of years of adjustment and adaptation passed before a burst of enthusiasm and splendor broke over the desert lands. Beginning in the 1780s impressive new missions sprung up on old Jesuit sites. Friars and soldiers closed ranks in probing the forbidding desert in search of reliable routes to the growing province of California.

The fresh hope that characterized the close of the 18th century was short lived, however. Within a scant forty years the whole venture approached collapse. Apache raids had ripped the northern frontier asunder; economic decline threatened the dependent mission system. And to top it all, Spain fell victim to the expansionist demands of Napoleon Bonaparte. As Old Spain crumpled under the emperor's heel, New Spain raised the cry of independence. Mexico was reborn. But the new political freedom only assured that the lack of funds and concerns would shrivel the frontier that belonged to a deceased empire. Northwestern deserts held no attraction for the sophisticated politics of the new nation.

The Anglo-Americans who entered this land in mid-nineteenth century were puzzled by the ruins of an obviously splendid civilization. They swiftly annexed the vast land of mountains, deserts, rivers, canyons, volcanoes and beautiful bays. Its history was vague; its monuments, massive; and its potentials were staggering and unfulfilled. No wonder myths and legends sprouted to explain these anomalies in the desert West. Modern history has been left the task of explaining to contemporary man that these desert lands have not always been a wilderness void of importance. Quite to the contrary, they have been the scene of history making events and the home of bold explorers who had opened new worlds to an empire already sated with discovery.

What modern America is learning about this land is not only that it has a fascinating history, but also that the visions of her pioneers were more realistic and perhaps even more challenging for our times than for theirs. The true treasures of the Pimería — her agricultural and recreational potentials, are still untouched. The curious thing about this land is not that it has had a history few have heard about, but that the past visions of her future are still unfulfilled. Kino would not be amazed at how much we have done, but at how little and how poorly we have dealt with this splendor of creation.

THE PIMERÍA ALTA:

FRANCISCANS AND AFTER

The sudden expulsion of the Society of Jesus by Charles III in 1767 stunned the world-wide Spanish empire. Jesuits were literally everywhere, doing everything, and their swift removal left simple folk and sophisticates confused and disbelieving because it happened without an issue and without warning. Charles III's unexplained, secretive order rocked every frontier in the Americas. Sonora and the Pimería Alta were no exception. But such are the decisions of absolutists. For decades the frontier missions had depended on religious missionaries for stability and direction. Entry and assimilation into Spanish society was not easy or automatic. Although the primary goal of the mission program envisioned the peaceful transition of native communities into full-fledged

José de Gálvez

Spanish towns, that transition came slowly and with difficulty. Not all loyal subjects of the Crown were as willing as the missionaries to wait for the social and cultural changes to take place because opportunities to exploit land and labor diminished the longer the missions held sway. When the decree of expulsion of the Jesuits came, many Spanish colonists cheered the news. In the name of the Enlightenment new freedom was finally being given the Indians. Others were appalled because they recognized the duplicitous program of the Bourbon monarch.

In New Spain the change of policy was championed by Visitador General José de Gálvez, one of the most trusted and influential friends of Charles III. His task was to spearhead reforms being pressed by the Bourbons of Europe. And in his estimation the Jesuits were the single most effective deterrent to those changes. Gálvez was consumed by hate for the Blackrobes whom he considered too powerful and too worldly. Far more to his personal liking were the men of the Order of Friars Minor, the Franciscans; their religious spirit and ascetical practices conformed to his idea of how religious ought to be after the reforms were achieved. The Viceroy, the Marqués de Croix, staunchly agreed.

When the decree of expulsion was issued, Gálvez and Teodoro de Croix, the viceroy's nephew, lost no time in enlisting the aid of Vice Commissary General Fray Manuel de Nájera to assign some fifty Franciscan replacements for the missions of the northwest. Nájera complied with Gálvez's directive because he really had no alternative. Little did he realize the devastating change in mission policy that Charles III and Gálvez had devised. In the fashion of the times Gálvez appealed to Nájera's predilection for purely spiritual administration. Temporal management of the missions would become a function of civil officials. Mission communities would become villages of Spanish citizens willing and able to pay taxes, traffic with Spanish merchants, and take their place in the new society.

Therefore, Nájera quickly sent orders to the apostolic colleges operated by the Franciscans in New Spain, asking for the requisite fifty men. Volunteers responded enthusiastically. By September, 1767, forty-seven gray and blue robed friars had gathered near Tepic for transfer to the northwest and Baja California. It would be a marvelous new epoch in mission history now that the entrenched enemies of God and Church (the Jesuits) had been dislodged. The missions of Sonora and the Pimería were waiting.

Gálvez had made it quite clear that the Franciscans were only to minister to the spiritual needs of native communities. They were to leave all temporal administration to other appointed Spanish officials. The mission lands were being registered in the names of individual Indians, entered on the tax rolls, and distributed among eager colonials. All the financial holdings of the mission societies were confiscated and given to the Royal Treasury. The Indians themselves were no longer obliged to a day or two of communal labor as had been their tradition since pre-hispanic days. Rather, they were only to work for pay, or not at all. They were to forsake their native languages and use Spanish alone. No longer were

Spaniards proscribed from living in mission towns, because totally free intercourse was now encouraged. Every Indian would be a completely free citizen of the new society. And the Franciscans' task was to make it all happen. This was not a simple case of substitution; it was wholesale upheaval just short of secularization.

THE FRIARS ARRIVE

By mid-winter the first of the friars from the Apostolic College of the Holy Cross at Querétaro had arrived in the Pimería Alta. The trip had been exhausting for many and the desert frontier was anything but hospitable. Fray Diego Martín García walked to San Ignacio; Fray Juan Díaz rode to Caborca. And Fray Juan Crisóstomo Gil de Bernabé went north to Guevavi. Gil and Díaz, as well as a later arrival, Fray Francisco Hermenegildo Garcés, each within a few years would pay with his life for the enlightened policies of Gálvez and Croix.

1768

Francisco Garcés

Throughout the first half of 1768 the rest of the Querétaran contingent arrived at their posts. Fray Joseph Soler took over Ati very close to his companion Fray Joseph del Río at Tubutama. Fray Joseph Agorreta tried his hand at the struggling mission of Sáric. And the hardest job of all fell to Fray Francisco Roche whose mission was Suamca, the most exposed to Apache incursions.

Santa María de los Pimas, or Suamca, was situated in a pleasant valley at the headwaters of the Río Santa María, later to take the name of the Río Santa Cruz. It had been the almost lifelong headquarters of the controversial Jesuit missionary, Padre Ignacio Keller. Keller had figured prominently in the disastrous Pima rebellion of 1751, so the mission had known the ravages of Indian wrath whether Apache or Piman. Roche's assignment to Suamca would be genuine front-line duty on a shaky frontier. It did not take long before he was put to the test.

An exemplary Franciscan, Fray Francisco took up residence at Suamca in June; the natives of the community were unimpressed by his commitment to poverty. Their desires lay in other directions. Sensing a discontinuity of purposes — probably due to the worldly influence of the Blackrobes, Roche retreated to Cocóspera for a brief period. By November, however, he bravely returned to Suamca where he was caught in a savage attack by Apache raiders. Luckily he escaped with his life, but Suamca never rose again from the ashes of its destruction. There was a message in all of this, but no one was listening.

Down river to the north Roche's companion, Fray Francisco Garcés, found San Xavier del Bac much to his liking. Moreover, the newly instituted policy of Gálvez was equally pleasing because he did not have to spend boring hours in the administration of the temporal affairs of the mission. Better to ride the trails of the western deserts than lock horns with neighboring Spaniards over Indian land and labor. Through the next decade Garcés stitched his name prominently in the fabric of history by crossing and re-crossing the trails of the western desert. His treks carried him beyond Yuma to the Mojave and northwest to California. As many have said, as a restless explorer he was the Franciscan answer to Padre Kino.

The Pimería, both Alta and Baja, put the apostolic mettle of all the Franciscans to strenuous test. By Gálvez's plan they had been stripped to near impotence in the administration of the missions. They were without means of discipline or encouragement. Each friar received 360 pesos annually from the King as his stipend. Although many had complained loudly that the Blackrobes had misappropriated their salaries to themselves, it became painfully obvious that the exiled missionaries had never been guilty of such accusations; in fact they had been marvelous managers in a decrepit and outmoded system that never corresponded to reality. Every member of the Franciscan replacement team complained bitterly to the college at Querétaro. Something would have to be done quickly or the whole effort would collapse as had many of the churches and conventos. For more than two years everything except administration of the sacraments was in the hands of civil commissaries – and they were the only ones profiting from control.

When the imperious Visitador General Gálvez finally returned to the mainland after a preposterous expedition to Baja California, he met missioner after missioner who pleaded for a change in policy. Even the megalomaniacal Gálvez had to agree. He relented by ordering that all the temporalities be returned to the control of the missionaries. Mission President Fray Mariano Buena y Alcalde breathed a little easier although he knew most of the moveable property had long since been carried off by the interim commissarios. With all his power Gálvez would be no help because he now lapsed even more frequently into demented raving; the incapacitating condition that plagued him in California only worsened in. Sonora. The desert's heat had not abated and the austerities of the frontier offered no solace. Fray Buena adroitly confined the Visitador to the mission at Ures where they tried to coax him to relax and recuperate. For several weeks Buena protected him from pressing correspondence and disturbing news. By late 1769 Gálvez was recovered enough to travel on to Chihuahua and Mexico City. Sonora was spared – at least for the time being.

POLITICAL CHANGES

The 1770s dawned amid profound political changes and rumors of more to come. The old familiar system of viceroys, kingdoms, and provinces was rewoven into an even more bureaucratic system of intendencias which had strong military overtones. Social and economic roles were streamlined to increase tax revenues and stress defense. Throughout Sonora and the Pimería Indian populations shrank with dread epidemics of contagious disease; peace was threatened in every sector. It was lucky for Gálvez that he was far distant because the situation might have snapped his mind permanently.

Charles III recalled the Visitador to Spain to take charge of the Council of the Indies. But Sonora still remained the focus of Gálvez's particular madness. From Madrid he promoted isolated, thorn-choked Arispe to the status of capital of the Provincias Internas, a regional jurisdiction newly created as something less than a viceroyalty. He conspired with Fray Antonio de los Reyes to accept consecration as the first bishop of Sonora although Reyes was at complete odds with his Franciscan brothers. No small wonder that the work of the quiet friars on the frontier has been overshadowed by the intrigue and machinations of men in power.

Colonization and frontier defense dominated the minds of the policy makers. Frontier communities were drawn into the tangled purposes of global strategy. Fray Francisco Garcés was ordered to search out an overland route to the newly established California outposts – missionary way stations along the military supply line to Monterey. Frontier-born Captain Juan Bautista de Anza rallied scores of hopeful ranchers and adventurers to join him in incorporating Alta California into rejuvenated plans for expansion. Under the leadership of friars and soldiers the long arm of empire stretched northward to counter the Russian and English advances in North America. Theoreticians of expansion planned new towns, new commerce, new economies, and new routes of transport; people were merely pawns in a game of dreams. Unfortunately for Fray Garcés, three of his Franciscan companions, and the dedicated Captain General Fernando Rivera y Moncada, the dream would become a deadly nightmare.

1775

An expansionist euphoria had enveloped most of the Pimería Alta. Missionaries and military were agreed that the Indian populace had at last come to terms with change. Henceforth all would be peace and prosperity. Teodoro de Croix, Caballero and Commandante General of the Provincias Internas, who ruled from Arispe in less than viceregal splendor, erected and erased presidial garrisons like a child with toy soldiers. And together with Fray Juan Díaz he designed a colony-mission on the banks of the Río Colorado – a place he had never seen, among a people he never understood. It was social planning gone mad.

MASSACRE AT YUMA CROSSING

Already the Yumas had grown short of food and supplies. How could they expect to refurbish expedition after expedition that braved the waterless deserts to cross the river where their ancient villages stood? The Spanish answer was simple and direct. A mission town would rise among the dunes. So, in the short daylight of December, 1780, long columns of Spanish immigrants reached Yuma crossing on the Colorado; the Indians perceived nothing but more problems. How were all these people and animals to be fed, watered, and housed? Where were the ever-present gifts by which other Spaniards had bribed their favor? Clearly these people had come to stay because straight streets aligned to compass bearings

1780

were laid out in the shifting sand. Yuma might never be the same again.

It was now a century after the tragic revolt of the Pueblos in New Mexico, and the Spaniards were pressing again. The natives took it for seven months. Then it became unbearable. In the sultry heat of July, 1781, the Yumas struck the unsuspecting Spaniards. Their two communities on either side of the broad river were totally destroyed. For a while the well known Fray Garcés was spared, but eventually all four Franciscan friars fell in the carnage. Angry hordes of Indians slaughtered the scattered platoons of soldiers; women and children were taken hostage. At any cost the Indians were determined to repossess their land and their way of life. It was a complete disaster. Over a hundred Spaniards lost their lives on the river where peace had reigned since Alarcón had first come two and a half centuries before and where Kino himself had dreamed of a prosperous mission to protect Indian interests and serve Spanish needs.

1781

Teodoro De Croix

Caballero Croix's essential link to California was severed. His social plan was a shambles. But he remained adamant that his unworkable schemes had only failed because of the incompetence of the friars and soldiers to whom he entrusted his programs. Still smarting from his reverses Croix left office in 1783 to accept promotion as the Viceroy of Peru; Charles III continued with his incredible record of rewarding paper politicians. As Croix left Arispe in viceregal splendor, Fray Antonio de los Reyes arrived in an episcopal pique. He had a plan for Sonora that was as unpopular and unworkable as Croix's approach to frontier defense had been.

The missions of the Pimería Alta succumbed to ecclesiastical intrigue during the administration of Bishop Reyes. The new Commandante General of the partially reorganized Provincias Internas, Felipe de Neve, hardly had an opportunity to redirect the scattered efforts of Croix before he died. The Intendent of Sonora, Pedro de Corbalán, continued to the best of his abilities to achieve peace and equilibrium despite the pressures of the reformers. Reyes soon moved away from inconvenient Arispe to opulent Alamos. The missionaries of the Pimería he simply absorbed into his new diocese in a confusion of policy and purpose. Following the orders of Charles III, who himself followed the suggestions of Reyes, the Bishop established the Custodia of San Carlos, a new administrative district that would institute reforms in the mission communities. Nearly to a man the Franciscans fought Reyes' plan. The ecclesiastical counteroffensive was headed up by Fray Antonio de Barbastro, who finally won out against the first Bishop. Perhaps it was because Charles III had died in the interim. Perhaps it was because Barbastro's arguments were clearly stronger. Who knows? But at least the missions and missionaries of the Pimería had entered a whole new phase of development by the 1790s. Bishop Antonio de los Reyes never saw the surge of growth; he passed on to his eternal reward at Alamos in 1787.

1787

One defiant Franciscan, Fray Juan Bautista de Velderrain, had determined that no ecclesiastical intrigue was going to deter him from building the finest church in the north. Velderrain had charge of San Xavier del Bac. And beneath the bishop's nose construction was begun on one of the most, if not the most, spectacular churches built during the period. Friars at Tubutama and Cocóspera, and later at Caborca and Tumacácori, caught construction fever; monuments in the desert grew upward despite fiery rhetoric and early opposition.

Nuestra Señora del Pilar y Santiago de Cocóspera presents a prime example of controversy on the Sonoran frontier. Although Bishop Reyes had championed the idea of his Custodia of San Carlos, the Franciscans loyally looked to the apostolic college at Querétaro for independent assistance. Essentially this was the squabble between the Vice Custodian Barbastro and Bishop Reyes. Querétaro obliged the requests of Barbastro and continued to find and send volunteers to the mission frontier. One exemplary friar was Juan Antonio de Santiestevan, theology professor turned missionary. Fray Juan had come to the frontier in the early days of Reyes' new custodia; he long outlived the controversial Bishop and transformed the humble Jesuit adobes at Cocóspera into a finely sculpted church of brick and embellished neo-classic design. When Santiestevan retired, he left an elegant church in the hands of Fray Joaquín Goitia. But Cocóspera like all the missions on the frontier was coming up on the hard times of Mexican independence. The system that had brought the missions into existence and nurtured them over the years would shrivel in the echoes of the "Grito de Dolores" when Mexico gained its freedom from Napoleonic dominated Spain.

Without doubt Fray Barbastro had won the battle of mission policy – at least ecclesiastically. His position as President of the Pimería missions championed the old ways of winning native souls with temporal inducements. Generally speaking, the missions that were less exposed to hierarchical interference flourished; the communities more exposed to secular control disintegrated. Barbastro thought quite simply "by their fruits you shall know them." These policies held sway until 1795 when the winds of change blew out of Mexico City and Querétaro once again. 1795 The breeze arrived in the form of Fray Diego Miguel Bringas de Manzaneda y Encinas, appointed Visitor General to restructure the administration of the northwestern missions. Bringas wafted in during the spring of 1795.

Bringas and the Unfiled Report

Despite his courtly name, Bringas was a native Sonoran. Born at Alamos in 1762, he had been too young to have known the Blackrobes' missionary policy. When he arrived again in Sonora with the powers of visitor, he set out quickly to discover the problems that had infested the far flung communities. Rumors were rife that the Grayrobes were sliding into ill conceived practices and that the missions were bordering on corruption. Bringas recognized the rumors for what they were – rumors – and criticisms born of greed and discontent. Nonetheless, he composed a striking report to King Charles IV which never reached the Spanish court. In it he appealed for a staunch return to mission policies as they had been constituted before the reforms of Charles III. For the Pimería he wanted each of eight mission stations to maintain two resident friars; he also wanted them to be operated as *reducciones* without the presence of Spaniards in the communities. And having visited the whole frontier of the Pimería he recommended the establishment of several new missions including one at the junction of the Gila and Colorado where the colony of Croix had been annihilated.

His task completed, Friar Bringas left the Pimería Alta in the able hands of Fray Francisco Iturralde, a veteran of almost a score years in the northwest. As President of the missions Iturralde tried valiantly to mend the torn fabric of charity among dissident friars. He struggled to advance the cause of the missions among the still military-minded colonial officials. In many ways it appeared hopeless, but progress slowly became evident. The closing years of the 18th century were hard ones because the Spanish empire was on the wane; English imperial ambitions waxed. France was ambivalent under Napoleon's nod. Who really could care for the needs of frontier missions when the purposes of power could be better served by war and the threats of war? Mission finance became even harder. Imperial policy sought out ever more stringent forms of taxation and revenue. President Fray Iturralde could only cringe at the absurd new demands to tithe the Indian communities.

1803

The last gasp of greatness in the Pimería missions came in 1803 when Fray Andrés Sánchez broke ground for an impressive new church at Caborca. The other mission communities had relatively decent churches and conventos. Only Tumacácori and Caborca were substandard by early 19th century reckoning. The plan at Caborca would be nearly a duplication of San Xavier del Bac – only slightly larger and with more utilization of neo-classical embellishments. Energetic dedication made it possible to complete the church before the unforeseen Mexican War of Independence in 1810. Lucky for Caborca, because Tumacácori's less pretentious structure was started later and work was suspended when imperial funds were cut off and local funds were exhausted.

1810

MEXICAN INDEPENDENCE

With the War of Independence the northern frontiers suffered economic and social strangulation. The subsidized economies of the mission communities shriveled. Military support and protection for the Indian programs almost completely ceased as loyalties divided and provincial factions vied for power. Precisely at the time the fledgling United States was consolidating power, New Spain was disintegrating as the Spanish empire crumbled under Napoleonic domination. To all intents and purposes the mission as an institution of social change ceased to function. Before its final disappearance the next two decades were denouement. The central themes of the drama had been played through; the principal actors were dead and gone. The few mission compounds that survived anywhere fulfilled only a custodial role in the decline of empire.

History pays attention only to the confusions of the struggle for power in Mexico and seldom treats of the collapse of the frontier. From 1810 onwards the frontier communities fought for recognition and identity. Loyalties were strained to the breaking point; support came from nowhere. The Franciscan college at Querétaro tried to maintain some semblance of commitment to the missions under its sway, but the college itself was plunged into political intrigue. Furthermore, the apostolic colleges had depended heavily on peninsular Spaniards to man the missions. In the search for independence most peninsulares were suspect, so the missions found themselves without financial subsidy or replacements.

When Mexico finally emerged as an independent imperial republic, there was a comparative period of stability. From 1821 through 1827 it appeared that the missions might regain their former strength. But a new spirit of nationalism swept through the people and the successful revolutionaries demanded the exile of all peninsulares. Few trusted the presence of the pure-blooded, Spanish-born immigrants. The decree of expulsion hit the ranks of the religious orders particularly hard because many of the missionaries had come from Spain; it meant the immediate abandonment of scores of mission communities. In a few instances some peninsular priests were allowed to remain because of age or ill health.

Sonora was one of those provinces whose missionary team was mostly Spanish. Only two friars were left to care for the vast desert land. It was an impossible task by any standard. The Mexican federal congress on December 20, 1827, passed a law expelling the peninsular born Spaniards from the entire country. The effect in Sonora was to reduce the missionary force to two friars: Raphael Díaz, a Spaniard with friends in Arispe, and Mexican born José Pérez Llera. What an incredible task for two! Pérez Llera remained at San Ignacio from where he administered

1821

1827

all of the western desert missions – Tubutama, Oquitoa, Caborca and all their visitas. The chain of missions along the northern route fell to Díaz who roved from Cocóspera to San Xavier del Bac, including the garrisons at Tubac, Tucson, and Terrenate. The Mexican law of secularization had the same effect on the missions as the Jesuit expulsion in 1767 because all the properties were confiscated by civil administrators. The two friars were bereft of all power and moneys, and thus the Indians were deprived of their help. It was a sad situation for the native population. Although some of the properties were returned in 1830, the essential damage had been done, and it was only a matter of time before the powerful military leaders of the north interpreted the laws in their own favor. The lands quickly fell into the hands of a very few families – a social phenomenon that has plagued Mexico for centuries.

1837

1841

Father Pérez Llera acted as mission president until 1837. He succeeded in doubling the missionary force from two to four. But the team of friars were old and powerless. By 1836 the assigned missioners had grown to six, yet these lasted only a few more years because Pérez Llera left the Pimería in 1837 as the winds of political change shifted once again in Mexico. The others either abandoned their impossible situations or died. By 1841 there were only two left once again. It was the beginning of the absolute end of the missions that were once so proud under Padre Kino.

THE PROBLEM OF SECULARIZATION

Mission history is decidedly more complex than it appears. The whole phenomenon of evangelization in the New World began in the Caribbean at the time of Columbus when the privilege of the *Patronato Real* was extended to cover the newly discovered lands. The Patronato Real bestowed on the King of Spain the power to appoint bishops throughout the Spanish empire in exchange for the Crown's acceptance of the responsibility to finance the churches. To some extent this was off set by the bishops' power to impose tithes on the diocese. Thus the *secular* clergy were granted benefices that paid for their personal and parish expenses.

When the lands of the New World were subjected to Crown control, there was no Christian population upon whom to impose the *diezmo*, or tithe. How would these churches be supported? The Crown quite simply paid the salaries of the resident ministers until such time as the churches became self sufficient – once thought to be not longer than ten years. The only clerical help that was available for these meager payments were the members of the religious orders, such as Franciscans, Dominicans, Augustinians, and later the Jesuits. And the native communities they served remained exempt from paying the tithes until they ceased to be missions. Since many missions rapidly became centers of productivity, tensions grew between the religious missionaries and the secular bishops who wanted to tax the Indians and displace the religious; thus secularization, that is, turning the churches over to the bishops, would ease the financial burden on the Crown and enrich the coffers of the regional church.

The missionaries, however, saw this as nothing more than a disguise to take over Indian land and labor. Consequently, a running battle ensued in which mission status was prolonged and secularization delayed. By the 18th century the problem had grown to significant proportions; royal officials were constantly complaining of payments to phantom missionaries in vacant posts. The religious explained away the Crown's enormous debt because of the lack of ministers in an overworked apostolate; the Indians were simply unprepared to assume full vassalage.

In the northwest of New Spain secularization made a marked advance in 1753 when the Jesuits turned over twenty-one missions to the diocese of Durango. For the most part, these were very old missions in the Sierra Madre Occidental and proved to be extremely difficult posts for the secular clergy who were not inclined to the austerity required to run the ecclesiastical parishes. Theoretically, the religious missionaries who were relieved of duty were to be assigned to new missions that would be established in the Pimería Alta and Colorado delta. It was a bold experiment that turned sour because several secular clergy opted to leave the struggling communities. And expansion in the north was interrupted by native rebellion among the Pimas and the coastal Seris.

With the expulsion of the Jesuits scores of missions were vacated, and few replacement religious were available, so many former missions defaulted to secular control. The story repeated itself inasmuch as there were no clergy available and the communities were too poor to sustain a parish priest. The churches reverted to diocesan ownership and the lands to Indian residents, who promptly found themselves liable for taxes from which they were previously exempt. Within a very few years the lands were confiscated by royal officials for being delinquent in the payment of taxes. The land was then "purchased" by unscrupulous colonial settlers, mostly among the military. Hence, secularization became the standard process for the seizure of Indian lands, revealing the immense power the mission system had wielded in protecting native land and labor.

When Mexico wrested its independence from Spain, the royal payments under the Patronato Real ceased, and the remaining missions fought for survival. Their effort was very short lived as Mexico soon imposed its own strict rules of secularization such that the long coveted agricultural lands fell into the hands of political appointees and the powerfully rich heirs of Spanish authority. Stability was defined as economic stagnation, when in reality it was only effective protection against greed.

Formal secularization of the missions of the Pimería Alta happened circumstantially. With the exile of so many Jesuits in 1767 and their replacement by only nine Franciscans, the mission communities without resident missionaries quickly fell prey to control by the Bishop of Sonora. That new diocese had very few secular priests, so the Franciscan Bishop, Antonio de los Reyes, tried mightily to conscript the Querétaran friars, who had been assigned to the various missions, into the Custodia of San Carlos, which was little more than a legal fiction on the road to secularization. Naturally the Querétaran friars resisted and they held out only to experience the expulsion of Spanish born clergy from the new nation of Mexico.

What few people realized was that the definition of secularization was changing with the times. At one time, the process had stood for the transfer of native *doctrinas* (missions) to the ministration by the secular clergy. Now the process was becoming more sharply focused on the confiscation of Church property which was handed over to officials of the State. This is why the problem of secularization confuses so many people. Just as one cannot glibly define a church as a mission, neither can one merely assert that secularization is the transfer of jurisdiction from religious to secular clergy.

Consequently, when we speak today of the "missions" of Padre Kino, we invoke a powerful time in history when missions were native communities administered by self-less missionaries for the sake of bringing the Indian communities into the then modern world. This is not to argue the good or bad of that process. It is only to say that missions were not simple churches built in the wilderness. They were a very intricate part of directed culture change, conceived of as a wholesome method to bring the Indian populace, singly and collectively, into the modern era.

Certainly Kino was proud of the Indians he served and he was confident of the zealous role they would play in the expanding frontier. He opposed exploitation throughout his life and championed the skill and talents of all the Indians he dealt with. Nothing he did fits the mold of modern criticism about paternalism and enslavement. No wonder he was so dearly loved by so many, and feared by so many others whose lives were consumed with a quest for wealth and power. So today, even though few adobe churches survive among the Kino missions, his name lives on, attached to imposing temples, crumbled ruins, and desert towns because his spirit is still alive in the Pimería Alta. The task of sharing the Faith and seeking freedom and justice for all is as demanding today as it was when he rode the desert trails trusting that God's "heavenly favors" would rain down on all those he served.

Favores Celestiales

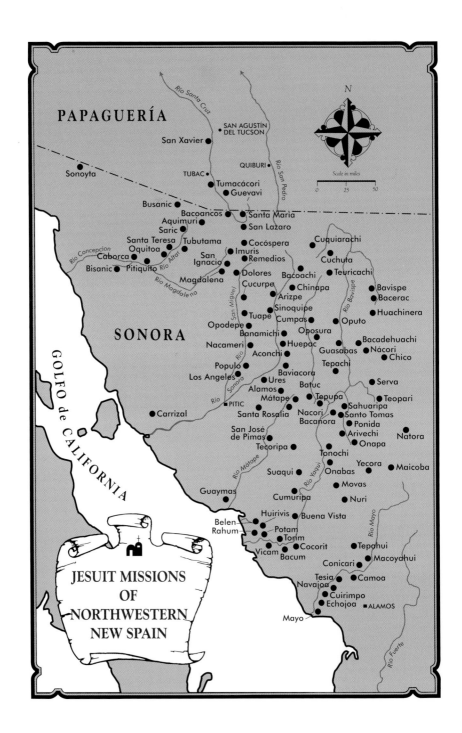

PAPAGUERÍA

Rio Santa Cruz

SAN AGUSTÍN
DEL TUCSON

San Xavier ●

N

Scale in miles
0   25   50

QUIBURI ●

Rio San Pedro

Sonoyta ●

TUBAC ●
Tumacácori ●
Guevavi ●

Busanic ●

Bacoancos ●   Santa María ●
Aquimuri ●   San Lazaro ●
Saric ●

Rio Concepcion
Santa Teresa   Tubutama ●   Cocóspera ●   Cuquiarachi ●
Oquitoa ●   San   Imuris ●
Caborca ●   Ignacio ●   Remedios ●   Cuchuta ●
Bisanic ●   Pitiquito ● Rio Altar
                                         Teuricachi ●
            Magdalena ●   Dolores ●   Bacoachi ●   Bavispe ●
Rio Magdaleno   Cucurpe ●   Rio Bavispe   Bacerac ●
                                  Chinapa ●
                         Arizpe ●   Huachinera ●
                    San Miguel
                         Sinoquipe ●
SONORA   Tuape ● Cumpas ●
            Opodepe ●   ● Oputo ●
                    Banamichi ● Oposura ●
         Nacameri ●   Huepac ●   Bacadehuachi ●
                    Aconchi ●   Guasabas ● Nácori ●
         Populo ●   ● Chico
GOLFO de   Los Angeles ●   Baviacora ●   Tepachi ●
            Rio Sonora   Ures ●   Serva ●
                    Alamos ● Batuc ●
            Rio   ■ PITIC   Mátape ● Tepupa ●   Teopari ●
CALIFORNIA   Carrizal ●   Nacori ● Sahuaripa ●
                    Santa Rosalia ● Bacanora ● Santo Tomas ●
                                              Ponida ●
                    San José   Arivechi ●
                    de Pimas ●   Onapa ●   Natora ●
                    Tecoripa ●
                    Rio Mátape   Tonochi ●
                         Suaqui ●   Onabas ●   Yecora ● Maicoba ●
            Guaymas ●   Rio Yaqui   Movas ●
                         Cumuripa ●   Nuri ●

                    Huirivis ● Buena Vista ●
            Belen   Rio Mayo
            Rahum ● Potam ●
                    Torim ●
                    Cocorit ●   Tepahui ●
            Vicam ● Bacum ●   Macoyahui ●
                         Conicari ●

JESUIT MISSIONS
OF
NORTHWESTERN
NEW SPAIN

                    Tesia ●   Camoa ●
            Navajoa ●
                    Cuirimpo ●
                    Echojoa ● ■ ALAMOS
            Mayo ●

Rio Fuerte

126

THE MISSIONS OF PADRE KINO

Contemporary Americans seldom question their stereotypical concept of the "Spanish mission." Some concepts are pious ones – of devoted religious, obedient neophytes, and quaint churches in the wilderness. Some are impious – of domineering clerics, enslaved natives, and fortress compounds. How does the historian disabuse anyone of these commonly held ideas that have sprouted in the darkness of ignorance? One important task of history is to enlighten the past so that present and future generations can know the genuine contributions our predecessors have made.

Although we speak of the "Spanish mission" or the "mission system," in reality each mission recorded a distinct, even diverse, history. The net-works of missions in different regions and in different epochs may have been analogous, but they were certainly not the same. In northern New Spain (Mexico) five or six systems can be described, although they each conformed to the *Laws of the Indies*. The "Kino mission chain" in the Pimería Alta was only a segment of one of these systems.

The first two, and earliest, systems were formed along the spine of the Sierra Madre Occidental. In the late 16th century Franciscan Friars opened mission centers among the Chichimec tribes while the Jesuit Blackrobes labored along the Pacific slope. Franciscan evangelization in the central plateau occasioned their entry into New Mexico where the Spaniards encountered the highly organized Pueblo societies. By contrast the Jesuit missionaries more commonly dealt with scattered nations in the rugged mountains and river valleys of western Mexico. In the late 17th century the Jesuits opened a new chain of missions in Baja California that required significantly innovative procedures for administration and supply. At the same time the Franciscans pressed eastward into Texas where their missions played a dual role in conversion and frontier defense. When the missions of Alta California were established in the late 18th century, the role of the mission had undergone substantial modification due to the secular goals of military security and overland supply. Nowhere at any time was there a uniform mission system.

Unfortunately too many writers have created romantic fictions about mission life. As the story typically goes, a stalwart, rugged man of God rides into the wilderness and with bare hands builds a monumental church on an idyllic hilltop. Curious natives respond to reverberating bells; songs fill the air; and fields of grain wave in the golden sun. The splendor and abundance are irresistible. The truth, however, was quite different. Usually the new missionary rode into long established native villages under military escort; negotiations ensued in which the Indians decided to accept or decline the invitation to have a European living and working among them. Only after long years of patient ministry was a missionary able to penetrate new frontiers and find new peoples who might be eager to accept him and the Faith. It was almost exclusively a matter of the missionary's established reputation.

Missions were also successful to the extent that the initial enticements of food, clothing, and supplies led to the richer benefits of education and incorporation into the comparative opulence of Spanish society. Indeed, the Spaniard saw the mission as a means of acculturating and pacifying fiercely independent peoples. The religious considered the mission as the only reliable stepping stone to salvation. The Indian saw the mission as a tolerable, if threatening, means to enter a new way of life. In other words, the mission was a complex social reality serving multiple purposes and perceived according to very different scales of value.

Some generalizations about Spanish missions are valid. In the case of the Jesuit missions there was a relatively consistent plan of organization and administration. All New Spain constituted a single, religious "province" which came under the jurisdiction of a single superior or "Provincial." Every member of the Society in New Spain was subject to his authority. For reasons of administrative, as well as religious asceticism, an individual Jesuit also answered to a local superior or "Rector." Frequently interposed between the Provincial and the Rector was a "Visitor" who held limited, delegated powers from the Provincial; this bridged the geographic gap between Mexico City and the far flung frontiers. Contrary to popular opinion, a missionary 2000 kilometers from Mexico City was not free to act independently. Even expeditions into neighboring lands required prior, explicit permission from the Provincial or the Visitor. Hence the chain of command in the Jesuit missions began with the missionary on the frontier who answered to the local Rector; the Rector, to the Visitor, and through the Visitor to the Provincial; the Provincial answered directly to the General of the Society in Rome, and in civil matters to the Viceroy.

San Xavier del Bac

The entire missionary sector was divided into "rectorates" that were responsible for clusters of missions. A particular mission often consisted of a "cabecera" or resident headquarters and several near-by "visitas" or mission stations – the distinction normally being in the residency status of a missionary. A rectorate, in turn, comprised several cabeceras. In this way the whole of northwestern New Spain's Jesuit missions were organized.

When Padre Kino came to the northwestern frontier of New Spain in 1687, he was building on the reputation and hard work of a half century of predecessors. His Blackrobe companions chose the site of Cosari for the new cabecera among the Pimas Altos. This new conversion was nothing more than the next stage in a long- standing plan of mission expansion. Kino did not ride in alone on horseback and dazzle the natives with linguistic prowess or magic. He rode in with well known missionaries who introduced him to the Indians, now eager to have their own resident European because they recognized from afar how the other villages had fared under Spanish dominion.

Padre Kino named his new post Nuestra Señora de los Dolores de Cosari. Although the initial name stood for only an individual mission station, it almost immediately became the cabecera of a series of small visitas, such as San Ignacio and Remedios. As acceptance of the missionary program spread rapidly through the Pimería Alta, Kino established new cabeceras where other Jesuits became the resident missionaries; Dolores soon advanced to the status of a rectorate with Padre Kappus as the first local superior. And in this sense we moderns look back at the whole of the Pimería Alta and call the twenty-odd missions of the rectorate of Dolores the missions of Padre Kino. He had something to do with all of them; he was remotely in charge of all of them; but, there were several other Jesuit missionaries immediately responsible for their care and development. And many passed into the hands of Franciscans at a later date – in other words, Kino in origin, Kino in spirit, and historic in evolution.

When Padre Kino rode the Indian trails at the turn of the 18th century, he selected many existent villages as sites for future missions. On the following pages several of these sites are described in word and picture. None of the imposing Spanish colonial churches still standing today, however, were the handiwork of Padre Kino himself. The splendid buildings at San Xavier del Bac, Caborca, and Tubutama represent the last flourish of Franciscan efforts in a land they inherited from the expelled Jesuits. All of these churches were erected nearly a century after Kino had established the first missions in these wide-spread pueblos.

Less than a quarter century after Kino's death most of the proud structures he had personally built with his team of skilled craftsmen were crumbling into ruin. Twenty years of scarce man-power and neglect

N.S. de la Purísima Concepción de Caborca

brought the churches to the brink of total collapse. When a new wave of missionary replacements arrived in the 1730s, each felt as though he had to begin again. And even their churches, constructed through the middle of the century have – for the most part – all disappeared or given way to newer, sturdier structures. It is all part of the saga of life – of birth, death, and resurrection.

Actually all that remains of the personal work of Padre Kino are a few deeply protected adobes inside the walls of Cocóspera and under the mounded ruins of Remedios. Until 1990 the lonely ruins of Dolores boasted of a part of the church sacristy with traces of plaster and pigment, but in that year the mighty bulldozer scraped away all traces. Even after centuries, opposition to Kino's presence was finding adherents. His own churches were proud buildings, constructed by Indian craftsmen under his continual supervision. Now they are only sad monuments to the ravages of weather, Indian wars, revolutions, and blindly ignorant treasure hunters. The little physical trace that remains today of Padre Kino's presence will soon disappear as each year the summer rains cleanse the savage wounds of metal detectors and shovels that have surpassed the frenzied destruction of mission sites by Apaches and senseless revolutionaries. But even the inexorable forces of change and decay will never touch the persistent memory of Kino and the men who catapulted this desert into the annals of history. Whether a humble Jesuit ruin or a magnificent Franciscan monument, the sites and churches of the Pimería Alta will always be the missions of Padre Kino who propelled the original communities into history.

To the person who takes the time to visit the missions of northern Sonora and Arizona will come the realization that the finest hours of life are spent in helping those in need. These great mission churches rose up in the desert because people had learned the value of cooperation, sacrifice, and dignity. If these missions continue to fall into ruin, the tragedy will not be the loss of the buildings, but the loss of the sense of human solidarity that men like Kino developed in the desert southwest.

NUESTRA SEÑORA DE LOS DOLORES

Dolores, mother mission of the Pimería Alta, was founded on March 13, 1687, when Padre Eusebio Kino decided to base his apostolic ministries at the Pima village of Cosari. The site of Dolores was a favorite ranchería among the Pimas, and under the guidance of skillful missionaries it promised to yield even greater returns. Although the first mission buildings were temporary, by 1693 there was a "good and roomy church with seven bells, well provided with vestments, linens, and altars; a water-powered mill, a carpentry shop, blacksmith shop, herds of cattle and oxen, horses, a farm, orchards, vineyards, and a winery."

Memorial cross for 300th anniversary of Kino's arrival

Despite this prolific effort Kino's interest and familiarity with other regions of the Pimería deterred him from making Dolores a permanent headquarters. His major efforts at construction were focused on more remote sites along the frontier, such as Caborca and Bac. Dolores was destined to return to the dust. Only ten years after Kino's death Jesuit reports speak of Dolores as unhealthful, humid, and cold; the church was falling to the ground. Many Indians had moved away and during the ensuing decade many of those who stayed died in recurrent epidemics.

By 1732 the mission was all but abandoned; too few people were living there to warrant restoration. The last resident priest was José Javier Molina who struggled valiantly to protect the Indian population from the dreaded smallpox epidemic. Then, Padre Visitador Jean Baptiste Duquesney noted in 1744 that the mission had been vacated.

The population of the San Miguel and Cocóspera river valleys had declined so drastically by 1748 that Padre Ignacio Keller consolidated the survivors at Cocóspera where he could serve them from his own station at Santa María Suamca. The decline progressed so rapidly that Dolores was only partly inhabited by 1750, formally abandoned in 1762, and defunct, for all intents and purposes, by 1763.

Dolores cemetery in nave of Kino's mission

Wandering Spanish colonials settled in the mission ruins during the later Jesuit period. They converted some of its buildings to new uses, and by the time the Pimería Alta came into the hands of the Franciscans, the buildings and lands had been made into a hacienda.

All that remains of Dolores today is the magnificent setting and a cemetery in the fallen nave – a melancholy; reminder of the glory that has vanished from the Sorrowful Mother of the Pimería Alta.

NUESTRA SEÑORA DE LOS REMEDIOS

Remedios, of all Kino's missions, was the reluctant one. No sooner had Padre Kino visited the village of Coágibubig in 1687 than the Pimas living there reneged on their acceptance of building a mission. But the padre's persuasive powers won out and within seven years a large church and living quarters were under construction. The mission compound rose in slow agony; the records continually refer to the church and quarters at Remedios as "nearly completed" for four more years.

By 1699 the walls were up and the roofing was to be begun, but torrential rains eroded the apse, soaked the adobe foundations and washed

Remedios' sanctuary wall in 1967

out the presbytery. The damage notwithstanding, the building was repaired, and in a few months the small church was useable. Once the initial structures were completed, Kino commenced work on two large and spacious churches, here at Remedios and at Cocóspera. Both churches reached completion at the same time and Padre Kino planned a whole week of celebrations to dedicate the two churches in January, 1704. With a few minor exceptions they were architectural reflections of one another. "Each church has a high cupola set on the arches of the two chapels which form the transept, and each cupola has a sightly lantern above and in the middle."

134

Unfortunately, both missions were built within range of frequent Apache raiding. Defense towers were added to the churches but these failed to protect the missions from the enemy's destructive attacks. After Kino's time the pueblo of Remedios dwindled in size and importance. Epidemics took their toll along with Apache arrows. The church was crumbling in 1723, in ruins by 1730, and totally abandoned before 1740.

Ruins of Cocóspera, Remedios' twin at the time of construction

Unlike Dolores over the rise to the south, Remedios never even became spoils for a future hacienda – everything of importance was gone. Even the vestments and church ornaments were transferred to Santa María Suamca for safe-keeping while a new mission was prepared among the Sobaipuris in the north.

Remedios is but a memory and a name which belongs to the hills surrounding it. The splendor of its church lives on only by comparing it to the decimated ruins of Cocóspera, its twin in construction and its survivor through time.

Nuestra Señora del Pilar y Santiago de Cocóspera

No church in northern Sonora has ever held the same degree of fascination created by the lonely ruin of Cocóspera. Situated on a high bluff above the picturesque Cocóspera valley, this mission has witnessed the rise and fall of empire. Apaches used the valley as a convenient route of invasion into the central Pimería. Recognizing the region as a natural staging area for defensive forays along the frontier, the Spaniards used it as a jumping off place for explorations. Its rich river lands provided the colonial residents with abundant produce, and the settlers, in turn, offered the numerous services and skills so precious to frontier life from the pueblo which grew up around the mission. After the collapse of Spanish imperial power the deserted mission-town became the home for remnants of French and American adventurers whose invasions of Sonora during the turbulent 1800's failed. Although a small town flourished here in the mid 1800s, it disappeared when travel north ceased to follow the river valleys and shifted to the lower route of the Guaymas-Tucson railroad.

The original church was the near twin of Remedios mission. Padre

Cocóspera's sanctuary pockmarked by treasure hunters

136

Kino laid the foundations for a large church with transepts and adobe arches. The inner walls of the ruin show clearly that the Franciscans built their church around the ruined shell of the Jesuit mission so frequently ravaged by Apache attacks. The facade of the Kino church was flanked by large, square defense towers which later formed the bases for twin bell towers. The windows and doors were constructed of posts and lintels with flat

Rubble below choir loft and main door

surfaced splays and wood-grill apertures. The interior walls were coated with a thin white plaster and decorated with red ocher paintings.

When the Franciscans renovated the mission in the late 18th century, they lined the adobe shell with fired bricks, raised strong, rock buttresses outside the nave, and erected a new brick and stucco facade. The church interior was faced with brick and heavily plastered, thus permitting an exuberance of raised plaster reliefs incorporating a variety of swags, urns, and scallop shells.

The mission ruin of Cocóspera is easily reached today by taking the Highway 2 from Imuris to Cananea. The site is located on the northwest side of the road. Perhaps it is too accessible because it has been continually ravaged by misguided treasure hunters whose pick-hammers and shovels have almost destroyed this monument to man and God on the desert frontier. For many years now the Mexican government has provided a caretaker to guard the ruins; who knows but one day lonely Cocóspera will be escorted to a new life by restoration?

SAN IGNACIO DE CABURICA

San Ignacio de Caburica, six miles up river from Magdalena de Kino, rests peacefully near some low hills around which the river veers on its southwesterly course from Imuris. San Ignacio is one of the true delights of the Sonoran mission frontier. In modern times the mission and village have been all but forgotten in the rush of business and travel.

San Ignacio, Kino's second mission

The mission site was chosen by Padre Kino in 1687 because Caburica was a populous Piman rancheria. A series of small chapels served as visitas or as temporary buildings until 1693 when Padre Agustín de Campos arrived to transform Caburica into a cabecera. His new church was burned during the Pima uprising of 1695, but soon rebuilt. For forty-three years San Ignacio served as the headquarters for Padre Campos, one of the longest terms of missionary service on record in the Pimería Alta. Quite understandably San Ignacio captured Campos' heart because of its central location and agreeable climate.

Campos' longevity and missionary skills made San Ignacio a training ground for new Jesuits moving into the missions of the Pimería.

Baroque door

Highly skilled in the various Piman dialects, his presence at San Ignacio naturally turned it into a language school and proving ground for those who would be assigned to other more distant churches. After Campos left in 1736, Padre Gaspar Stiger filled the same role of teacher and superior until his death in 1762.

Although the rector of the missions did not always reside at San Ignacio, the Pimería Alta was effectively administered from this location throughout the post-Kino period, or roughly until the expulsion of the Jesuits in 1767. The early years of Franciscan administration were dominated by the centrality of this mission, but as westward expansion overtook the Pimería, San Ignacio deferred to the more northerly and westerly missions of San Xavier del Bac, San Pedro y Pablo del Tubutama and La Concepción de Caborca. When the whole northern frontier was consolidated into the diocese of Sonora in 1779, San Ignacio drifted into oblivion. Today the pueblo is a jewel of tranquillity.

No thorough architectural investigation of San Ignacio has ever been carried out, but evidence indicates that the present church is reminiscent of the style employed by the Jesuits in the Pimería. Padre Stiger built a completely new church here in 1753, and church records imply that this structure was merely renovated and remodeled in subsequent years. Both Franciscan and secular

Caracol stairs

priests undertook extensive remodeling, but comparative study shows that the bell tower, size of the nave, and the circular, mesquite-log staircase were characteristic of the earlier churches of the Pimería.

San Pedro y San Pablo del Tubutama

A visit to Tubutama is to relive the missionary past – but without missionaries. Although the pueblo is well off the main highway, it is accessible by paved roads. From any angle of approach the town looms up like a welcome oasis in the desert, dominated by the squared towers of a white mission church. The church fronts on a plaza that is frequently void of cars or trucks; usually one or two horses stand in the shade of local cantinas. A pervading silence is broken occasionally by the voices of children at play or by a burro train clopping through the streets.

In 1687 Padre Kino was invited to Tubutama. Immediately, he began construction on a small church and mission visita. The struggling new mission was later the scene of the outbreak of the Pima rebellion of 1695. The mission itself was burned out and the crops destroyed. But it was only a short while before the repentant Indians repaired the damage and Tubutama took its quiet place in the history of the Pimería. As isolated as the town now seems, Tubutama served as the jumping off station for the bold crossings of the Papaguería that had to be undertaken to explore the western deserts.

Tubutama before restoration

Tubutama, old interior

After Kino's time manpower was at a premium and Tubutama only occasionally and temporarily had a resident priest. By 1730, however, more men were sent as missionaries into the Pimería, and Tubutama was raised to the level of a cabecera at which time a new church was erected. Padre Jacob Sedelmayr, another famous Jesuit explorer, built a church here at mid-century. But it came to grief during the 1751 Pima rebellion when Luis of Sáric burned the church and murdered several residents of the pueblo. Once the rebellion was quelled the church was again rebuilt; a decent structure was reported here by Padre Manuel Aguirre in 1764.

When the Franciscans took over in 1768, the mission enjoyed a favored place in the Pimería and a new, more elaborate church was built here in 1788. This is the same structure that graces the pueblo today. Recent repair and restoration have paid strict attention to the earliest known details so that the church today remains a fine example of what it once was. The older mission buildings were apparently closer to the river bluff than the present church, but all trace of them has disappeared. In the early 1950s a group of American adventurers, searching for the fictitious Jesuit treasure, nearly dynamited the pueblo. Fortunately the men were stopped in time or another masterpiece of colonial architecture would have crumbled in tragic ruin.

Another stunning change at Tubutama was the construction of Cuatemoc Reservoir, damming up the ever flowing Altar River where mission fields once flowered.

SAN ANTONIO DEL OQUITOA

Arriving in Altar, one never gets the impression it was at the junction of two major Sonoran rivers. Irrigation projects and deep water wells have so altered the flow of water that only a wary traveler would suspect how the terrain looked in colonial times. The nearest village up river from Altar is the quaint community of San Antonio del Oquitoa. A

San Antonio de Oquitoa

simple, lonely church surmounts a rounded hill above the town; its stark lines are surrounded by a sun-seared cemetery.

Oquitoa was never an important historical site even in Padre Kino's day. What fame it had was infamous because residents of this town were the murderers of Padre Saeta in Caborca. But now Oquitoa has taken its quiet place in history and has become a favored spot along the Kino mission trail.

In 1980 restoration work was completed on the then decaying church. Fascinating discoveries were made of earlier construction techniques and decorative details. Now San Antonio del Oquitoa has taken a position of pride in the history of Sonora. The narrow nave, thick adobe walls, and beam ceiling remain as one of the last vestiges of a truly bygone era. Oquitoa doesn't seem very different today from what it must have been in the 18th century.

Rarely in Jesuit mission country does one encounter a church under the patronage of Franciscan saints. In the case of San Antonio del Oquitoa it appears that the patron of the village was chosen because the first resident priest in the Altar valley was Padre Antonio Arias at Tubutama. Soon after his appointment Oquitoa became a visita in his care. It is curious how strongly history is written in the traces of unassuming names.

SAN DIEGO DEL PITIQUITO

In the days of Padre Kino, Pitiquito was never a very important pueblo although he frequently visited there. For years it remained a dependent mission station of Caborca. In 1772 Fray Antonio de los Reyes, later the first bishop of Sonora, reported that there was no church at the site. The Franciscans began the present structure in 1778; since then, the church has undergone extensive modification.

The history of Pitiquito has been vague at best. In the early months of 1967 the residents of the town became terrified at what they thought were the appearances of spirits in the church. Skeletons, eyes, hands, and words emerged and vanished on the massive white-washed walls throughout the interior of the church. The more timorous people interpreted these words and figures as omens predicting the immediate end of the world.

But on investigation it was found that the ladies of the town had been cleaning the church for a fiesta. They used detergents to wash the walls. And a day or so after each cleansing, figures and words would appear on the surface. What no one knew is that the whole church had been decorated with large liturgical and doctrinal murals, but the paintings are so old that not even the oldest resident had the faintest recollection of ever seeing the church with anything but a

San Diego del Pitiquito

white-washed interior. A request has been made to the Mexican federal government to attempt to restore the murals since they could well become the best example of catechetical art known for this period of Sonoran history.

La Purísima Concepción de Nuestra Señora de Caborca

Deceptively peaceful, Caborca rises along the banks of the Río Concepción at the heart of an amazingly fertile plain in the great western desert of Sonora. Padre Kino himself was impressed by its potential and began constructing a new mission here in 1693. He entrusted his hopes for the mission's future to Padre Francisco Xavier Saeta, but the Pima rebellion of 1695 demolished those hopes with the murder of Saeta and the pillaging of the village. Caborca, however, recovered and for a half century grew in importance as the western staging area for explorations into the Colorado delta.

But Caborca's calm was shattered again in the Pima rebellion of 1751; this time the blood of Padre Tomás Tello stained the sands of the agricultural heartland. Again peace returned to the broad valley and the agricultural economy pulsed with new importance. Although one might suspect that such an isolated place would eventually experience peace, it did not; violence broke out in 1857 when Henry A. Crabb and his fili-buster army besieged the townspeople in the mission church. His ill-fated attempt to seize northern Sonora ended in the execution of his entire force on the mission steps. Residents claim that the bullet marks on the facade date from this historical episode.

The present church was built between 1803 and 1809. It shows many architectural similarities to San Xavier del Bac. A large convento once stood to the north of the church but raging floods in the early 20th century ripped into this construction and

also eroded away the sacristy and rear of the sanctuary; it happened again in the 1980s. The Mexican government has since restored the church and made it a national monument. Caborca is less remembered for being an important mission and the scene of two martyrdoms than for its being the place where American expansion into Mexico was halted by the bullets of Sonoran patriots.

A new plaza was created in front of the church in 1967. The small archway which serves as the formal entrance to the plaza was made from the stone facade of an ancient chapel in the town of Batuc which has been inundated by the waters of El Novillo dam on the Río Yaqui. In 1997 the plaza was greatly expanded.

SAN CAYETANO DEL TUMACÁCORI

Tumacácori's past is elusive. All the maps of Padre Kino indicate an Indian village of Tumacácori on the east bank of the Santa Cruz River. Apparently the site was a convenient crossing place where the waters of the river had a chance to broaden out. From Tumacácori the trail crossed the river to the west and continued on down to San Xavier del Bac. Actually the Pima settlement of Tumacácori gained importance only after the establishment of the presidio of Tubac in 1752. Prior to this, the main concentration of Indians was at Los Angeles de Guevavi, an extensive mission some twelve miles up river. In many ways the early history of Tumacácori is the history of Guevavi. Guevavi, like Tumacácori, was an original Kino visita, but a major mission complex was not built here until

Aerial view of Tumacácori showing granary and mortuary chapel

after Kino's time, in 1732 when Padre Johann Grazhofer took charge.

Exactly ten miles south of Tumacácori was also located the mission visita of Calabasas. Throughout Jesuit times there was nothing more here than a small wayside chapel, and its importance varied with the shifts in Indian population. It seems that because of recurrent Apache raids the Sobaipuris pulled out of the San Pedro river valley and took refuge at these missions within the sphere of Spanish protection.

Since the present mission bears a different name, San José de Tumacácori, than the one Kino chose, it is most probable that the church was erected on a new and somewhat different site from that of Kino's. Archaeological investigation has revealed a structure immediately east of the present church and most probably represents a Jesuit period church that enjoyed protection from the Tubac presidio (after 1752). The present mission was erected in 1773 and refurbished at various times. Construction on a larger church was begun in the opening years of the Mexican War for Independence and suspended in 1822 due to the lack of funds from royal coffers. Nevertheless, the church remained in use until secularization became fully effective in the 1840's. Mexican utilization of the property for mining activities gave rise to later American speculation that the mission was the scene of clandestine mining by Catholic clerics.

Tumacácori is now the headquarters for the Tumacácori National Historical Park. The site originally came under Park Service control in 1908 when it was made a National Monument; and it was raised to full park status by an act of Congress in 1990.

LOS SANTOS ANGELES DE GUEVAVI

Situated on the Guevavi Ranch on the east bank of the Río Santa Cruz are the last traces of Arizona's oldest Jesuit mission, Los Santos Angeles de Guevavi. The site was selected by Padre Kino in the early 1690s because of its centrality to the scattered rancherias of the upper river valley. Through the first years of its existence it was known variously as San Raphael Archangel, San Gabriel Archangel, and finally as Los Santos Angeles; no one could remember which patron was foremost anymore. Its first resident missionary was Padre Juan de San Martín who arrived in 1701; but the mission was soon abandoned and not until 1732 did Guevavi again host a resident priest.

Guevavi circa 1960

Although reconstructed after the ravages of the 1751 Pima rebellion, Guevavi's fortunes waned and by the last quarter of the 18th century it was reduced to a visita – often exposed to Apache raids and too far from protection by the garrison at Tubac. Graves of several prominent Sonorans, as the wife of Juan Bautista de Anza, were located in the nave, but all have been destroyed by avid treasure hunters. The National Park Service now has custody of the site.

THE VISITAS OF THE SAN PEDRO, SANTA MARÍA AND ALTAR RIVERS

Curiously the most scenic sections of the Sonoran border are rarely seen by tourists or even residents of the region. The natural causeways of communication in colonial times were the river valleys that are now avoided by modern transportation. Hence the splendors known so well to the men who made history in the Pimería Alta are enigmas to us who have come so suddenly upon the complex past. We travel different trails in faster vehicles along topographically altered highways.

The lower reaches of the Río San Pedro were studded with short-lived rancherias and potential visitas. The Apache menace drove the Sobaipuri Pimas from their traditional homes and eliminated the potential for conversion. To the west over the Huachuca Mountains, the upper portion of the Río Santa María (now the Río Santa Cruz) boasted a cabecera at Santa María Suamca (near Lochiel) and visitas at San Lazaro and San Luis Bacoancos. But a furious attack in 1768 obliterated the village and mission at Suamca. Then, the weakened condition of the Opata-Sobaipuri villages contributed to the collapse of the defensive perimeter along the Pimería Alta frontier. Over exposed and under staffed, garrisons at Terrenate, Tubac, and Altar were unable secure the frontier

Visitas along the Altar River present a similar history. Some of the them along this reliable water course rose to full mission status only to fall back again into ruin. A case in point is Santa Theresa de Atil, or Adid. Whatever the proprieties of the name, the place was made famous by Padre Ignaz Pfefferkorn in his classic *Description of Sonora*. When Pfefferkorn worked there in 1756, traces of the Kino chapel were still visible because the place had been by-passed in the rebellion of '51. Atil fell on hard times after Pfefferkorn was transferred to Cucurpe. Apaches raided it frequently; missionaries refused to minister to its flock, and eventually the vestments and church furnishings were lost.

Farther up the Río Altar, the important town of Sáric, was a mission for a short while. Now the people dispute where the mission might have been because its last vestiges have been so badly mistreated and forgotten. The same goes for Tucubavia, Búsanic, and other ephemeral villages along the ancient riverway.

SAN XAVIER DEL BAC

The foundations for the great mission of San Xavier del Bac were laid in 1700 by Padre Eusebio Kino. He had been impressed some years before by this largest of the Pima villages along the Santa Cruz. But even after the mission was completed, it remained vacant throughout the first decades of the 18th century. The first resident missionary Padre Francisco Gonzalvo fell terribly ill and died of pneumonia at San Ignacio the following August, 1702. With the shortage of missionaries in the north-

Facade of San Xavier del Bac

west, Bac remained vacant until 1732 when the Swiss nobleman, Philip Segesser attempted to re-gain lost ground. Even Segesser's stay was brief because he had to leave to care for his companion, Padre Grazhofer, who was deathly ill at Guevavi. With Grazhofer's death in 1733, Segesser split his time between the two missions. But illness felled him as well and Bac was taken over by yet another Swiss missionary, Padre Gaspar Stiger. Stiger stayed until 1737 when he moved south to replace the elderly Padre Campos at San Ignacio. San Xavier del Bac was then turned over to José Torres Perea, who lasted for two years until 1741. The isolation and distance from Spanish assistance made the post particularly difficult and dangerous.

The sequence of mission churches at Bac has long been disputed because of the incompleteness of the record. Kino's first church was be-gun here in April, 1700, and he monitored its construction throughout the first decade of the 1700s. Whether completed or not, no church was reported here in the 1720s. It would appear, however, that some edifice served as a church during the residency of Segesser, Stiger, Torres Perea, and Francisco Paver, who arrived in 1750 just prior to the Pima Revolt of 1751. During that ominous time the mission of San Xavier was pillaged and burned.

Bishop Granjon's entry gate from Tucson

Following an interlude of a couple of years, Padre Paver tried his luck again at Bac. He was back in 1753, but he determined it was wiser to operate out of Guevavi where there were still remnants of a mission. In late 1755 Padre Alonso Espinosa, a native of the Canary islands and recent missionary at Caborca, was transferred to Bac. He came in the auspicious company of the new Governor of Sonora, Antonio de Mendoza. While campaigning in the north in 1756, Mendoza stopped off at San Xavier to lay the cornerstone of a new and capacious church, which Espinosa worked on over the next several years. The foundations of this historic building lie forty yards west of the present church.

St. Francis Xavier

Espinosa's large adobe structure was the same one utilized by the Franciscans when they took over in 1768 from the exiled Jesuits. It served as headquarters for Fray Francisco Hermenigildo Garcés until he was transferred to Tucson to be in close support for the newly constructed presidio. In 1777 San Xavier was placed in the hands of Fray Juan Bautista Velderrain, who looked after the mission while Garcés explored routes to Alta California.

Bac's history has always been fascinating because it has always housed the largest Indian populations. For centuries it has been the meeting place and training ground for the hechiceros, medicine men, of neighboring tribes. From here Kino sent out messengers to learn about the peculiar blue shells which figured so prominently in the discovery that California was not an island. Kino dreamed of moving his headquarters to Bac, but the lack of men to assume responsibilities at Dolores made the move impossible.

Today, mission San Xavier del Bac is one of the colonial art treasures of America. Its baroque architecture is a monument to the splendor of the European civilization that first came to the desert frontier of Sonora and Arizona. Surrounded by fields of grain and cotton and by the adobe dwellings of the Papagos, it is a page from the past that has been forgotten in the haste of freeways and the waste of crowded cities.

THE MISSIONS OF THE LOWER GILA
AND COLORADO RIVERS

The Indian pueblos along the Gila bore a litany of apostolic names but to call them missions is to raise them to a dignity beyond the reality. At most, they were visitas for the missionaries of San Xavier del Bac, San Pedro del Tubutama, Santa María Suamca, and Los Angeles de Guevavi. Yet they have been traditionally so de-emphasized that their existence as visitas has been overlooked.

From the time of Padre Kino these pueblos were considered as potential missions and were to be visited whenever possible. Mission maps for the entire first half of the 1700s depict the chain of villages. There was continual contact, first with Kino, then Campos, and down through the years by Padres Ignacio Keller, Jacob Sedelmayr, and quite probably Gaspar Stiger and Alonso Espinosa. They were certainly attended by the Franciscans, most notably Fray Francisco Garcés.

It is nearly impossible to imagine the meaning of the Gila and Colorado missions today. The villages and their Indian populations have long since disappeared just as the shallow-draft steamers that once plied the desert river waters. But in the days of the active missions of the Pimería they were outposts on a frontier that strained toward California, the last havens of supply for the men who were penetrating the "Moqui" lands to the north and west.

The central pueblo along this coveted chain was San Dionisio, roughly identifiable with present day Yuma. The melodious Christian names of villages that ran upstream from San Dionisio are gone; San Pedro and Pablo, San Thadeo and San Simón have given way to Dome and Wellton. Thus the modern American frontier has erased any memory of these ancient sites where the Gila Pimas and Cocomaricopas met the Cross and Crown.

The shorter chain of missions down the Colorado among the Yuman peoples bore the names of the patrons of Spanish royalty – Santa Isabel, San Félix de Valois, San Casimiro. But none of these pueblos reached any significant level of development until long after the Jesuit expulsion in 1767. In the last quarter of the eighteenth century the misguided policies of Teodoro de Croix, the governor of the northern provinces, spelled an end to the missionary hopes enkindled here by Padres Kino and Campos.

De Croix's policies were a direct attack on the mission system. He wanted instant integration which amounted to sudden slavery for the Indians along the Colorado. Fray Francisco Garcés, O.F.M. tried valiantly to continue the expansion of the missions, but his policies crumpled under the "enlightened" guidance of De Croix. The Indians of the Colorado saw clearly through the Spanish colonial plan for them. So they rose in revolt in July, 1781, massacring some fifty Spaniards including Fray Garcés and Captain Fernando Rivera y Moncada, the military commander of Baja California.

The Jesuit visitas along the Colorado by then had disappeared with the shift of Indian population centers, and the Franciscan missions were now burned to the ground. The Yuman nation maintained stiff resistance to Spanish conquest and the mission system never revived in the river delta.

The falling facade of Cocóspera

THE MISSIONS AS OTHERS SAW THEM

BY THOMAS H. NAYLOR

The buildings that today comprise the "Kino chain of missions" stand witness to the inexorable forces of time. Whether from neglect or abandonment to the harsh physical forces of the Sonoran Desert, or due to a royal decision from Madrid to exile and replace an entire religious order with another, the churches have under-gone rebuilding and continual change. While some of the monuments have slowly eroded back into the earth, most of the buildings have seen periods of reconstruction and remodeling – right up to the present day.

Each church is unique as to its community setting, particular history, and the amount of interest and concern it has been shown. Lacking a protective community to care for it, Cocóspera has been ravaged by man and the elements to a near formless ruin. Only very recently has it been given any protection. Other Pimería churches have succumbed entirely. San Ignacio, Oquitoa and Tubutama have always enjoyed the care and protection of the small but immensely proud villages nestled at their feet. Shunted aside in the wake of the agro-boom, Caborca's mission church nearly fell total victim to flood erosion. Rescued because of its nationalistic importance as the scene of a Mexican victory over invading *norteamericanos*, the lost sections have now been rebuilt; the restored church and convento appear on the way to becoming a museum.

San Xavier del Bac found itself in the United States after 1853. That fact, and its proximity to heavily traveled routes in and out of Tucson, placed it in the limelight. Subsequently, a succession of church funded projects and state and federal assistance has beautifully preserved it. Being the finest example of Spanish colonial architecture in the U.S. has not hurt San Xavier. Both Tumacácori and Guevavi, also in Arizona, have fared much worse. Considerably less impressive and already in varying states of ruin, Tumacácori was eventually saved from oblivion by the National Park Service, but only mounds and fragments of walls mark the site of Guevavi today.

The visual record of the Pimería churches begins in the middle of the 19th century in the form of drawings and sketches. Among the best are those of J. Ross Browne in 1864 and Alphonse Pinart in 1879, examples of which appear in the following pages. The earliest photographs date from the 1870s and are relatively plentiful after 1900. Their quality and condition vary considerably. In the views that follow every attempt was made to include those that were most skillfully made and which most dramatically document the ever-changing churches through time.

SAN XAVIER DEL BAC

Taken probably in 1884, this view by H.T. Watkins shows the mortuary chapel and wall intact. Only two of the *estipite* columns have fallen from the portal decoration. *Courtesy of the Arizona State Museum*

View from "Grotto" Hill prior to the 1887 earthquake. *Courtesy Arizona State Museum*

The mission restored and landscaped circa 1950.
Courtesy Arizona State Museum

"San Francisco" in west chapel before restoration

J. Ross Browne drew this somewhat exaggerated sketch in 1864.
From *Adventures in Apache Country*

Taken sometime around 1913, the photo shows the attic above the
facade fallen. The roof was restored to the nave in 1920.
Robert Forbes, Arizona Historical Society

San Ignacio de Caburica

Dimwiddie posed people in front of
cemetery wall in 1894.
Courtesy of Smithsonian Institution

Side altars have
statues from old chapel
in Magdalena

Artifacts dating back
to 1683 are guarded
in a small musuem.

SANTA MARÍA MAGDALENA

J. Ross Browne's 1884 sketch shows the present church
and Campos' chapel apparently toward the right.

The sketch by Alphonse Pinart in 1871 distinctly shows the Campos'
chapel in front of and to the right of the present church.

An unidentified photographer took this photo around 1900 showing
the *espedaña* and *estipites* missing from the facade.
(perhaps due to earthquake damage in 1887?)
Courtesy Southwest Museum, Los Angeles

Courtesy Southwest Museum, Los Angeles

SAN PEDRO Y PABLO DE TUBUTAMA

An unknown photographer took this photo around 1900 showing a weathered church and barren plaza. Note the two small towers over the facade which were removed shortly afterwards.
Courtesy Arizona State Museum

Note attempt to imitate marble cornices with vegetal painting. Taken in 1935, the church was stripped of furnishings for protection against anti-clerical desecration.
Grant, Western Archaeological Center

SAN ANTONIO DE OQUITOA

The haunting church and cemetery on the hill above Oquitoa were thoroughly restored in the 1980s.

Interior showing mesquite beam ceiling and ocotilla cross ribs.
Courtesy Western Archaeological Center

Much of the convento was still intact until floods in 1908 tore them away. The architecture is very similar to San Xavier del Bac.
Courtesy Arizona State Museum

Located at the bend of the Río Concepción, the mission has been repeatedly damaged in successive floods through the 1980s.

Severe damage to sanctuary prior to restoration

THE DISCOVERY OF PADRE KINO'S GRAVE

From time immemorial history has explained the monuments of man's changing achievements. But in modern times man achieves change so rapidly that his links to the past are lost in the pace of change itself. History is no longer enough. So in recent decades man has developed the skill to search the ruins of his past to bring greater meaning to his present. The science of archaeology and the art of history have become as significant as astronautics and bio-physics because they create the perspective of man's cultural and scientific growth.

In this way the tiny town of Magdalena de Kino in Sonora, Mexico, is as significant as Guaymas with its satellite tracking station. Here in Magdalena in May, 1966, a team of anthropologists and historians located and identified the grave of Padre Eusebio Francisco Kino. The successful discovery climaxed nearly forty years of frustrating failures to identify the grave site.

When Herbert E. Bolton, as a young historian, published his translation of *Kino's Memoirs of the Pimería Alta* in 1919, he speculated that Padre Kino's remains had been transferred to San Ignacio de Caburica. Or at least that's what the local rumor of the time held. But in the meanwhile, the burial registers of San Ignacio were discovered, and in them Padre Campos carefully recorded where he had buried Kino in the chapel of San Francisco Xavier in 1711. Apparently Bolton and Professor Frank Lockwood probed the foundations of the present church in Magdalena around 1928, hoping to find Kino's grave. At least that's how the story is told today. By the time Bolton published his renowned biography of Padre Kino, *The Rim of Christendom*, in 1936, he dropped any mention of Kino's transferal to San Ignacio. The entry that mentioned Kino's burial in the little chapel of San Francisco Xavier stood as the single, reliable record of history about his grave. But where was that grave? In fact, where was the chapel? Indeed, where was the town in 1711? Unknown to almost everyone was Bolton's own opinion. Writing to Professor Lockwood, he told him he would "walk over the Padre's grave as he approached the church of Santa María Magdalena."

Many Mexican anthropologists and historians had tried to discover the obscured grave. Serapio Dávila in 1928 undertook an extensive search. He opened trenches in front of the present church and found the cemented foundations of an old parochial structure. Soon his workers were uncovering hordes of scattered bones, part of an old cemetery. How would one ever tell Kino's grave from any other? Dávila gave up.

Through the decades of the 30's and the 40's Professor Eduardo W. Villa, Rubén Parodi, Professor Fernando Pesqueira, and Señorita Dolores Encinas devoted their talents to solve the mystery of the missing site. But each effort ended in failure. New theories and newer rumors arose to explain the failures, thus creating only more confusion. In 1961 *Arizona Highways* dedicated their March issue to Padre Eusebio Kino – 250 years after his death in Magdalena. The state of Arizona was justly proud of its pioneer padre, and the circumstances of the dedication rekindled the same perplexing question: where was Kino's grave? In a gesture toward solution Editor Raymond Carlson incorporated into the issue an article by Donald Page in collaboration with Colonel Gilbert Proctor. The article focused attention on a complex of private dwellings on Calle Pesqueira some four blocks distant from the present church. Old timers called the place, "La Capilla." Indeed the structure looked like a chapel with its arches, niches, and scalloped passageways. Beyond what he had written Donald Page could not be consulted about his reasons for thinking this was the chapel of San Francisco Xavier; Page was dead. Colonel Proctor remained firmly convinced this was the authentic site.

Former failures to find the grave and new rumors reinforced each other until the residents of Magdalena could sit idle no longer. The grave should be found! In the late spring of 1963 the Magdalena Lions' Club obtained the permission of the Villa family to excavate the rooms of their family home on Calle Pesqueira; this was the erstwhile La Capilla. Curiously, the searchers found a subterranean tile floor, broken through in three places as if a coffin and two boxes had been removed through it. The rubble from the hole contained an old shoe, some beer bottles, and a cigarette lighter, indicating the hole had probably been refilled in the late 1920's. Many interpreted this discovery as evidence for the removal of Kino's remains (for protective custody) during the religious persecution of President Calles' regime.

Olvera's conceptual drawing of the Magdalena church
and Campos' chapel

A slow, careful investigation was then begun in the summer of 1963 by the Reverend Charles Polzer, S.J., to evaluate the findings of the Lions' Club project and to sort rumor from fact. With the help of Dr. William Wasley, resident archaeologist of the Arizona State Museum, it became evident that the excavation of "Proctor's Chapel," as La Capilla came to be known, were inconclusive at best. In fact, everything pointed to this site's being wholly incorrect. If true, then Kino had never been there to be removed!

Further historical investigations were undertaken in 1964 by Father Polzer. They were conclusive: the Proctor site was false. An archaeological survey of other Kino mission sites in the Pimería further corroborated Polzer and Wasley's objections to the validity of the Proctor site. But the discovery of the unusual openings in the tile floor of the "chapel" convinced the people that Padre Kino's bones had been carried off to safety decades ago. Rumor persisted and Magdalena was a maze of conflicting opinion.

While preparations for sculpting of the Kino Memorial Statue neared completion, the search for Kino's grave was shelved. In February, 1965, the nation was introduced to the prominence of Padre Kino by the unveiling of his statue in the nation's Capitol. Little did the people responsible for the statue realize what they had wrought concerning the discovery of Kino's grave. Mexico, too, was justly proud of Padre Kino; the Mexican people were not about to forfeit their share in Kino's fame.

Hence, at the request of Mexican President Diaz Ordaz, the Secretary of Public Education, Agustín Yáñez, commissioned Professor Wigberto Jiménez Moreno, the director of the Department of Historical Investigation of the National Institute of Anthropology and History (INAH), to find the remains of Padre Kino. It was June 30, 1965. Whatever legal log-jams the Americans conjectured over in the search for Kino's grave were swept away by the executive order of the Mexican federal government. Professor Jiménez Moreno, Dr. Jorge Olvera, the colonial art historian, and Professor Arturo Romano, the physical anthropologist of the National Institute, began a systematic search of the archives for information about the grave.

A quick trip to the Sonora frontier in August, 1965, acquainted Jiménez Moreno and Olvera with their newly inherited problem. Rumors and opinions varied on all aspects: the grave, the chapel, the remains, and their transfer. Professor Jiménez Moreno retired to Mexico City profoundly aware he had more on his hands than a casual search. Dr. Olvera remained behind to begin the methodical excavations which eventually crisscrossed the site of the ancient pueblo.

The traditional Fiesta of San Francisco forced an interruption of work in October. The trenches were back-filled and the investigators took advantage of the recess to evaluate their problem. Professor Jiménez Moreno accurately reassessed the situation. The discovery of the grave and the verification of the remains of Padre Kino would be no simple matter. The ingredients of success would be men and knowledge, both archaeological and historical.

It was April, 1966, when the team arrived again in Magdalena. Jiménez Moreno invited other qualified investigators to join the team. Padre Cruz Acuña from Hermosillo pitched in to comb through old diocesan archives and to interview old timers. The Reverend Kieran McCarty, O.F.M., historian of San Xavier del Bac (Tucson), signed on as research historian; his familiarity with Franciscan records aided materially in piecing out the fate of the old chapel. Dr. William Wasley was placed on detached service from the Arizona State Museum; his keen knowledge of the archaeology of the region provided the team with essential knowledge and skills. The chemist from the local clinic, Dr. Gabriel Sánchez de la Vega, gave invaluable service as the man most acquainted with the recent attempts to find the grave.

To the men of Mexico City in 1965 the search for the grave of Padre Kino appeared to be a simple matter. To the same men on the scene in Magdalena in 1966 the search was recognized as enormously complicated, and perhaps impossible. Excitement charged the air of Magdalena as the experts challenged the unknown.

Professor Jiménez Moreno understood his problem well. Here was a situation that required solution by a process of elimination. Units of the team spread out from Magdalena to probe each site favored by certain rumors and opinions. No reasonable possibility was overlooked, but one by one they were being eliminated as archaeological and historical evidence piled up. Slowly the circle of probability narrowed to

The team confirms the discovery, May 1966:
L to R: P. Santos Saenz, W.W. Wasley, Jiménez Moreno, J. Olvera, J. Matiella, and E. Burrus, S.J.
Not shown; P. Kieran McCarty, OFM,
A. Romano, and G. Sánchez de la Vega.

the plaza in front of the Magdalena church. Over two kilometers of exploratory trenches wandered through the town. Work crews exposed foundations of buildings long since forgotten. The earth yielded the bones of countless human beings.

It seemed as though the search would succumb to the intricacies of its own method. Then, the breaks began to come. The historians were building up key clues about the chapel from the archives. The major find was a description of the little chapel of San Francisco Xavier in an 1828 report by don Fernando Grande:

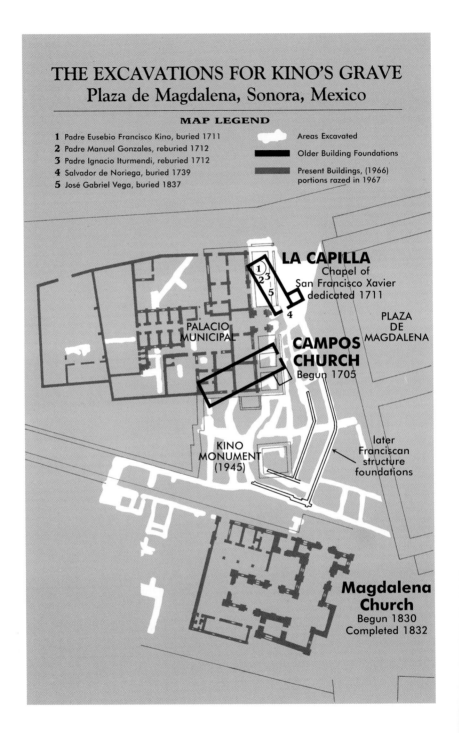

THE EXCAVATIONS FOR KINO'S GRAVE
Plaza de Magdalena, Sonora, Mexico

MAP LEGEND

1 Padre Eusebio Francisco Kino, buried 1711
2 Padre Manuel Gonzales, reburied 1712
3 Padre Ignacio Iturmendi, reburied 1712
4 Salvador de Noriega, buried 1739
5 José Gabriel Vega, buried 1837

Areas Excavated

Older Building Foundations

Present Buildings, (1966)
portions razed in 1967

LA CAPILLA
Chapel of
San Francisco Xavier
dedicated 1711

PLAZA
DE
MAGDALENA

PALACIO
MUNICIPAL

CAMPOS
CHURCH
Begun 1705

KINO
MONUMENT
(1945)

later
Franciscan
structure
foundations

Magdalena
Church
Begun 1830
Completed 1832

The chapel of this town is moderate. It is of adobe material. The entrance faces south. There is a moderate little tower in which are located three bells and another small one. It has nothing that draws particular attention. The principal and only altar is in the chancel. On it are set an image of the crucified Christ and another of the Virgin of Dolores; at the feet of the larger carving is the littler one of ordinary quality. And in some niches which form a reredos along the wall of the altar are set the statue of St. Magdalene, the patron of the pueblo (it's small but well carved), one of St. Francis Xavier, and one of Blessed Joseph Oriol; the latter is imperfectly carved. Midway in the nave of the church is a niche where there is located in a case a large carving of St. Francis Xavier, an object of devotion everywhere in the northwest. It is a beautiful and serious sculpture.

From the burial register two more relevant facts were learned. In 1739 a Spaniard, Salvador de Noriega, was buried at the entrance to the chapel. Nearly a century later a ninety year old Indian resident, José Gabriel Vega, was buried before the niche of St. Francis Xavier.

While the historians read through miles of micro film and dusted off old records, the archaeological teams followed the clues exposed by their trenching. The cement foundations in front of the church which had occupied Dávila years before were soon discounted when it was learned that lime was not used for construction in the Pimería during the earlier Jesuit period. Traces of adobe walls became more evident as the work crews learned the difficult art of distinguishing an adobe foundation from the alluvial deposits natural to the terrain. One wall which ran east and west had attracted the attention of Dr. Olvera who felt that it maintained the proper orientation shown in some mid-19th century sketches of the pueblo. But what is one wall in the middle of a whole town?

Dr. Wasley convinced the team of the need to correlate their findings with known Jesuit ruins in the Pimería; this was a stratagem worked out a year before between Wasley and Polzer, who insisted on the utility of the uncontaminated ruins at Remedios. On the very day Wasley, Olvera, and Romano were making their reconnaissance, the workmen in the trench that followed Olvera's favored wall came to its end. Professor Jiménez saw that they had really reached a corner. The wall turned toward the

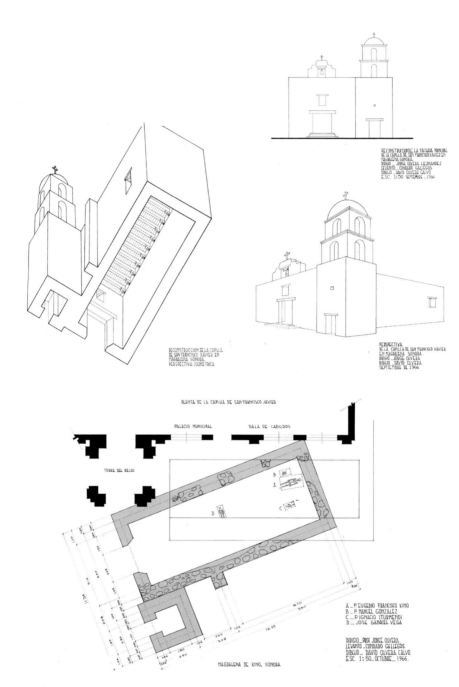

RECONSTRUCCION DE LA FACHADA PRINCIPAL
DE LA CAPILLA DE SAN FRANCISCO XAVIER EN
MAGDALENA SONORA.
DIRIGIO _ JORGE OLVERA HERNANDEZ
LEVANTO _ CONRADO GALLEGOS
DIBUJO _ DAVID OLVERA CALVO
ESC 1:50 SEPTIEMBRE _ 1966

RECONSTRUCCION DE LA CAPILLA
DE SAN FRANCISCO XAVIER EN
MAGDALENA SONORA.
PERSPECTIVA ISOMETRICA.

PERSPECTIVA
DE LA CAPILLA DE SAN FRANCISCO XAVIER
EN MAGDALENA SONORA.
DIRIGIO _ JORGE OLVERA
DIBUJO _ DAVID OLVERA
SEPTIEMBRE DE 1966

PLANTA DE LA CAPILLA DE SAN FRANCISCO XAVIER

PALACIO MUNICIPAL   SALA DE CABILDOS

TORRE DEL RELOJ

A _ P. EUSEBIO FRANCISCO KINO
B _ P. MANUEL GONZALEZ
C _ P. IGNACIO ITURMENDI
D _ JOSE GABRIEL VEGA

DIRIGIO _ PROF. JORGE OLVERA
LEVANTO _ CONRADO GALLEGOS
DIBUJO _ DAVID OLVERA CALVO
ESC 1: 50 _ OCTUBRE _ 1966.

MAGDALENA DE KINO, SONORA

Perspectives of Campos' Church.

City Hall. This was the first clear indication that it might define the foundations of a building.

Earlier in the exploration a crew had followed a lateral trench from Olvera's wall. Close to the north-south axis of the main trench they exposed a skeleton which Professor Romano identified as that of a European. Everyone regarded the discovery as "Suspect Number One." But then other pieces of the puzzle began to fall into place. "Suspect Number One" was on the south side of the adobe wall, and now that the long adobe wall to the east of the burial had turned a corner westward, there was little doubt that the Number One Suspect was Salvador de Noriega.

The east wall of the building showed evidence of a small buttress about midway. This corresponded to another historical discovery that Padre José Pérez Llera in 1828 erected a buttress to prevent the wall from further slumping! The corner discovered on the day the team was reconnoitering other missions proved to be that of the apse of the chapel. Cautiously the crews followed the line of the adobe and boulder foundation. The sharp spades cut through the soil ever so carefully. A shovel full of earth spewed into the screen. Nothing. Then at the base of the trench fell a piece of a skull, dislodged from the edge! A cry! Tension mounted as Dr. Wasley, Dr. Olvera, Dr. Romano and Professor Jiménez Moreno carefully exposed the whole skull. Could it be? Could it really be Kino's? It was 4:45 on the afternoon of May 19, 1966.

The entire team concentrated on the complex of trenches that seemed now to be located on the site of the ancient chapel. The skeleton discovered that fateful afternoon was delicately uncovered. The earth within the entire chapel area was cautiously peeled back. Then the key elements began to fall in place without complication. "Kino" was an original burial on the Gospel side of the chapel; the body had rested between the second and third foundation support, just as the burial record of Padre Agustín de Campos said. Then, at Kino's feet, but closer to the west wall, appeared a "secondary burial," one that had been transferred from another place. Across the chapel floor area, on the Epistle side of the apse, another secondary burial was uncovered in the packed earth. Fantastic! But predictable if this were really the chapel. In 1712, one year after Kino's burial in the chapel, Padre Campos transferred the bodies of Padres Iturmendi and González from Tubutama and interred them in the same

Fr. Polzer views Kino's remains, 1970

chapel on the Epistle and the Gospel side respectively.

Midway down the body of the church the excavators came upon another burial of a very old Indian man. Another key slipped into place because ninety year old José Gabriel Vega was buried before the niche of St. Francis Xavier which itself was located half way down the nave! And Salvador de Noriega was still lying patiently at the southerly entrance.

Professor Romano carefully studied the skeleton which lay on the gospel side of the building – if this were really the chapel. The man had been in his 60's. Kino had been 66. The skull was a classic European type from the Alpine region. Kino was from the Tyrol. The tibia bones of the legs showed a pronounced retroflexion. This was characteristic of the mountain people of Kino's homeland. When Wasley and Olvera removed the last traces of the wooden coffin which had caved in on the chest of the skeleton, they found a small bronze cross lying on the clavicle. This was typical of the Jesuit missionary of the 17th century.

On May 21, 1966, the team reached the conclusion that it had in fact discovered the long lost remains of Padre Eusebio Francisco Kino. On May 24 the announcement was made to the general public; no doubt remained in the minds of any of the team or the experts called in after the initial conclusion was reached. Rev. Ernest Burrus of the Jesuit Historical Institute at Rome, who luckily was visiting in Tucson, agreed in full. And finally on July14, 1966, the Academy of History met in Mexico City to review the evidence. Professor Jiménez Moreno presented seventy-two depositions explaining the discovery. Then, Dr. Alberto Caso in the name of the Mexican Academy of History pronounced in favor of the

Bronze cross

identity of the remains. Padre Kino was found at last.

As with everything that man does, there are always those who doubt. Some wanted the archaeologists to uncover a plaque or headstone. None ever existed, particularly for a man like Kino. He died as he had lived, in poverty and in the presence of his Lord. What the doubters had forgotten was that the monument over his grave was not just a headstone, but a chapel, and not just a cross with a name, but a whole culture.

So conclusive is the evidence which the team under Professor Jiménez Moreno uncovered that if the skeleton had been marked with another name, the anthropologists and historians would have realized someone was trying to play a joke.

But perhaps the most remarkable thing of all is that when the anthropologists were asked to reconstruct the likeness of Kino from his skeletal remains, they shrugged and pointed to a sketch on the wall of the City Hall. There hung the drawing done by Mrs. Frances O'Brien of Tucson. One could hardly come any closer to the human reality. She had sketched his portrait from the salient features of the Chini family as they lived in this century. She had only hoped to approximate Kino's likeness. Little did she know she had drawn the last clue in the recognition of Padre Eusebio Kino.

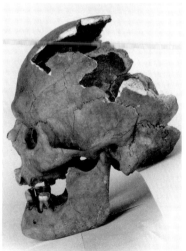

Kino's skull, 1966

THE PADRE KINO MEMORIAL PLAZA

The discovery of Padre Kino's grave in 1966 only set the stage for change in Magdalena. Hardly had the discovery team completed its work before Professor Wigberto Jiménez Moreno suggested that the town be officially renamed "Magdalena de Kino" in the Mexican fashion of commemorating her heroes. Kino's remains could not be left unprotected from the weather or unguarded from the curious and devout. Jiménez Moreno also urged some suitable memorial be designed.

The tiny population of Magdalena had inherited a whole new set of problems that were going to require cooperative efforts to solve. Scientific technicians from the University of Arizona's Department of Anthropology were invited to treat Kino's bones with special preservatives. The soil underneath was impregnated with plasticizers to stabilize the grave site. Covered by a metal roofed shed, a sealed glass vault encased the remains that were left *in situ*.

Patiently, the mayor at the time, Gerardo Nava, looked from his office door on the final resting place of Kino. Streams of visitors passed beside the excavations and impeded the efficiency of operations at city hall. What were the city fathers to do with the grave of a prominent hero at their doorstep? Nava smiled and opened negotiations to move all of the city offices three blocks away to the old Palacio Municipal, which was now serving as one of the city's schools.

So it was that Magdalena waited while federal, state and local officials pondered the proper solution. The care of the grave site passed on to the Instituto Nacional de Antropología e Historia, who designated Gabriel Sánchez de la Vega as chief custodian. Meanwhile the architect Vicente Medel visited Magdalena and devised some initial plans for a monument. The Governor of Sonora Lic. Luis Encinas Johnson, appointed a six man committee of Magdalena citizens to oversee the acquisition of property for the planned monument and to direct the demolition of buildings. Magdalena was on the move.

Then a group of prominent Magdalena citizens, who also served on the Comité del Monumento del Padre Kino, appealed to the Mexican federal government for a change in plans in the development of the Kino monument. Acquiescing to their desires, the government referred the project to the new Governor of Sonora, Faustino Félix Serna. He initiated a completely new plan – more comprehensive, more ambitious and more in accord with the local situation. Subsequently, the architect, Francisco Artigas, who distinguished himself in the colonial restoration of Guanajuato, was invited to design the Plaza of Padre Kino in Magdalena.

Artigas' problem consisted in the integration of several architectural features. The grave was not to be touched; the church was to be remodeled; and a site for a museum and library were to be included. His solution focused each element on a sunken octagonal fountain, thus achieving integration with simplicity and balance. The entire fifteen acre plaza was enclosed by portales (arched, beamed walkways) reminiscent of 18th century building design.

While the details of construction were being worked out, the Comité in Magdalena began the difficult task of relocating the many

Church and Crypt during construction, 1970

Portales that surround the plaza in Magdalena

families who lived in the affected area. Homes the inhabitants considered ancestral were to be leveled for the plaza. With an admirable sense of civic pride, and not without sacrifice, these families moved into newer houses provided in other parts of town. Over 7,000 square yards of buildings were removed to prepare for new construction.

Who paid the bill? Everyone seems to ask. The citizens of Magdalena, individually and through civic groups, contributed over one million pesos toward the ten million peso project. The rest of the financing came through matched donations from the federal and state governments. Cooperation was the key to the Plaza's creation.

In January of 1970 the Constructora Federal de Escuelas Públicas (CAFPCE) began work under the direction of the engineer Francisco Fernández. The restoration of the church was given over to the engineer Juan José Lecanda. Using local materials and labor, architect Gustavo Aguilar from Hermosillo pressed completion of the entire complex by December of the same year.

Before the Plaza was begun, the future president of Mexico, Lic.

Luis Echeverría Alvarez, visited Magdalena in December, 1969. Expressing his admiration for the gigantic labors of Padre Kino in advancing civilization in northwestern Mexico, he solemnly promised to return to inaugurate the memorial plaza. He kept his promise on May 2, 1971; a finished plaza and a proud population awaited him. At noon that day the newly elected President of Mexico visited the crypt while peals of applause welled from the "Pimalteños" who knew their President shared the enthusiasm of their heritage.

More than thirty years have passed since that hot afternoon in May, 1966, when an unexpected fragment of Kino's skull tumbled into the trench of weary searchers. From that moment on, custodians have stood at his grave, day and night. After some ten years had lapsed, the archaeologists noticed that the formaldehyde preservative so cautiously applied in 1966 was wearing thin. Like all humans Kino was turning to dust. Nothing could effectively be done in Magdalena to reverse the process of nature, so officials of INAH sliced away the hardened earth under Padre Kino's skeleton and masterfully encased him in a shock-proof shipping crate. Instead of riding hundreds of hard miles by horse, Kino returned to Mexico City by jet! In a few short weeks the painstaking treatment of the bones was finished and Kino returned to his earthly resting place. At least for the foreseeable future he was not going to crumble to dust.

The domed crypt cloaks a sudden surprise for the casual visitor who may utter a quiet word while looking down at the exposed remains. The architects shaped the crypt and dome to make a perfect contained megaphone so that even whispers can be heard all around the crypt – eliminating the need for guides to use microphones! And often when a visitor approaches the crypt from the sunken plaza, he will see Kino's determined face reflected in one of the windows. This was the clever design of Nereo de la Peña, a Mexican muralist from Caborca who painted the Rivera-esque scenes of Kino's life around the inside of the dome. His artistic talents have even migrated back to Segno, the town of Kino's birth, where Peña decorated the plaza and new museum with murals.

Kino's crypt

Magdalena de Kino now guards the mortal remains of the Padre on Horseback. More splendor than Kino ever knew on the desert trails of the Pimería Alta surrounds him in the plaza that bears his name. He was a man who enjoyed good art and good architecture. He was proud of the churches the Indians had built at Dolores, Remedios and Cocóspera. And he thrilled at the sight of hundreds of his friends coming across the deserts to share in celebrations. Normally drowsy and quiet, the plaza in Magdalena for countless decades has filled with pilgrims to the place where he was buried. First a humble chapel next to Campos' church; next, a separate chapel with a small bell tower; then, nothing but a delapidated ruin shaken by earthquake and rubble under a haughty town hall. The protective architecture had vanished, and Kino lay hidden beneath an ornamental orange tree. Yet, the people kept coming to Magdalena, ostensibly to visit "San Francisco."

One can only wonder how Padre Kino feels now, centuries later, when thousands continue to visit this latest monument erected in his honor.

Karsch photo of Silvercruys' statue

THE STATUES OF PADRE KINO

Statues are made of storied men, but seldom are stories written about statues. This, however, is the story of a storied man and several statues that honor him. The man who first considered Kino an apt subject for monumental art was Father Manuel González, then rector of the mission at Oposura. When Kino was conceiving his great expedition to the Colorado in 1700 to prove that California was not an island, Father González wrote him: "If you accomplish this, we must erect to you a costly and famous statue. And if the way is short, there will be two statues." The way to California was not short, but the accomplishments of Kino's career have already merited him many more than two statues.

The state of Arizona decided to honor Father Eusebio Francisco Kino in 1961 when several Arizona legislators introduced a Joint Memorial (N°. 5) asking that the Congress of the United States accept Padre Kino as the subject for the state's second statue in the National Hall of Statuary. Padre Kino had by that time already been recognized as the state's first pioneer, explorer, and cartographer.

The statue proposal and resolution created new problems because the regulations for statues in the National Hall do not permit purely imaginary conceptions of historical persons. Since the only reputed portrait of Kino was burned in the San Francisco fire of 1907, and no other known portrait of Kino existed, the unusual procedure was devised of creating a likeness from photos of family descendants, using salient and recurrent features. A special committee, designated by Governor Paul Fannin, began an intensive search for a portrait artist. To everyone's satisfaction they commissioned the renowned Tucson artist Frances O'Brien to portray Kino as he may have looked.

Once the portrait was submitted and accepted by the special Kino Memorial Statue Committee all the other pertinent facts about Kino and the dress of his times were compiled into a brochure which was distributed to all sculptors who cared to enter the competition arranged by the statue commission.

From a field of twenty-six entries the committee narrowed the competition to two finalists: George Phippen and Madame Suzanne

Silvercruys. Both of the "competition" statues displayed exemplary skill, remaining faithful to O'Brien's composite portrait, but the rendering of Padre Kino by Baroness Silvercruys conveyed more elements of the historical personage. The committee decided in her favor.

The half-size, plasticine model was shipped to Connecticut where Madame Silvercruys maintained her studio. There she began the complex task of fashioning a seven-foot version of Kino for the National Hall of Statuary. But the attraction of the desert and the figure of Kino brought her frequently to a studio in the foothills of the Catalinas where refinements to the features of the full-sized image were crafted. Finally, molten copper from Arizona mines soon flowed into the precision cast, and Father Kino emerged to take his place among the great founders of this nation.

On February 14, 1965, the first statue of Father Kino was unveiled before a crowd of seven hundred dignitaries from all over the nation and the world. The dedication ceremony took place under the Capitol Rotunda on the same spot where the body of President John F. Kennedy, who had signed the bill admitting Father Kino into the National Hall, had lain in state. It had taken two hundred and sixty-five years, but Father Kino was honored in the way Father González had predicted at the turn of the eighteenth century!

Father Ernest Burrus, S.J., from the Jesuit Historical Institute in Rome, summarized the significance of Kino in his dedicatory address:

Frances O'Brien painting EFK

We can feel justified in dedicating this statue not merely to the memory of one man, however great he may be; we dedicate it to all Americans who would share Kino's high ideals, lofty aspirations, and his bold vision of the future to bring together all peoples in true understanding and in an abiding communion of spirit; we dedicate this statue to the citizens, present and future, of Arizona whose pioneer founder he was; we dedicate it to our neighbors of Mexico, especially to those of Sonora who have preserved his memory in such deep affection; we dedicate it to Kino's native land and to the people and region from which he came; we dedicate it to the peoples of the lands of his adoption, whether in Austria, Bavaria, or Spain, where Kino spent so many of his intensely active years; finally we dedicate this statue of Father Eusebio Francisco Kino to all peoples and to all nations of good will and of high ideals.

These final, ringing words of praise, dedicating the statue, were not final at all. The Mexican delegation realized that Father Kino was more than an Arizona pioneer; he was a symbol even centuries later of the friendship between nations and the dreams of future prosperity. In a matter of weeks the President of Mexico, Gustavo Díaz Ordaz, ordered the grave of Father Kino to be located so that a fitting memorial could be erected to this giant of the Americas.

The tale of discovery constitutes one of those marvels of modern history and archaeological science. Even though no portrait of Kino is extant today, the discovery of his remains

Baroness Silvercruys with models

Martinez Sketch, 1966

in Magdalena has enabled scientists, employing techniques of physical anthropology, and artists to reconstruct his likeness with amazing accuracy.

Realizing the importance of Father Kino to the Mexican-American frontier, Governor Luis Encinas Johnson of Sonora commissioned a famed sculptor in Mexico City to depict Kino on horseback. Don Julián Martínez made a careful study of the skeleton of Kino discovered in Magdalena and formed a powerful figure in bronze to match the man who conquered the desert trails. Two statues were cast. The first was erected in Hermosillo, the capital of Sonora. It now stands at the far northern entrance to the city, dominating the panoramic landscape of the San Miguel and Sonora river valley.

The second statue was presented by Governor Encinas to the Governor and people of Arizona. The spectacular bronze statue was dedicated on the lawn of the capital in Phoenix in an impressive all Spanish program.

Now a statue of Father Kino stands in each capital as a symbol of a common heritage from the man whose dedicated life brought civilization and hope to a previously unknown frontier.

The Arizona dedication ceremonies included a unique look both backward and forward in time. By placing a "time capsule" in the base of the statue Arizonans reviewed their land as it was

Detail of Phoenix statue

190

known to Father Kino, as it was known at the time of the dedication, and as they predicted it to be 272 years from then. It was 272 years before the dedication that Father Kino first set foot in Arizona.

With the dedication of the second statue Padre Manuel González's prediction seemed to be fulfilled. But the gentle padre had miscalculated the ardent appreciation of generations of "Pimalteños." Don Julián Martínez privately confessed that the classic equestrian portrayal of Kino he had done at the request of Governor Encinas was done too rapidly. Despite the excellent quality of his research and his masterful creation of Padre Kino, he felt uncomfortable that he had not captured the soulful essence of the Jesuit missionary. He had sculpted the figure of Kino according to anatomical evidence from the grave; but this was not the younger, vigorous Kino whose visions had transformed the northwest.

J. Ivancovich inspects Hermosillo statue

Having completed an equestrian statue of Pancho Villa at the request of the President of Mexico which was presented to the City of Tucson, Martínez yearned to do another Kino because he had learned to love the courageous missionary explorer. And the time was right. In 1987 Arizona and Sonora would celebrate the 300th anniversary of Kino's arrival to the Pimería Alta. What better way to celebrate than to craft a new equestrian statue? But how should the new statue depict Padre Kino? And how could sufficient funds be raised? Martínez conferred with three Jesuits – Fathers Manuel Pérez Alonso, Gabriel Gómez-Padilla and Charles Polzer – and Jorge Olvera. Their stimulating meeting resulted in a decision to portray Kino as a younger man, truly an explorer who would ride the harsh, exhausting desert trails, but still a man of stamina and inspiration. Olvera insisted on conducting a thorough search for authentic tack for the horse and accoutrements for

the garb of the "Padre on Horseback." Martínez was emphatic that the statue capture Kino's spirit, vision and lofty idealism. Polzer then suggested that all these issues might be resolved if Padre Kino were to clutch an abalone shell in his hands as a symbol of the moment when all Kino's aspirations coalesced in his efforts to reach the abandoned peoples of California. In a matter of weeks Martínez created an intriguing maquette of a resilient missionary-explorer on a tired horse.

Kino at north entrance to Hermosillo

The eighteen inch model was completed just prior to Pope John Paul II's historic visit to Arizona. Why not present his Holiness a small memento of the first missionary to the Pimería! Craftsmen at the Desert Crucible, a Tucson foundry, cast the maquette in white bronze just in time for church dignitaries to present him with the statue of a deeply spiritual man about whom he knew nothing! So impressed with the figure of Kino, the Pope changed his prepared remarks, which had lauded the lone missionary so familiar to many, Fray Junipero Serra. Now there was new depth and meaning to the history of the church

Maquette presented
to the Pope

in the West; thousands assembled to hear the pontiff were astonished to hear him speak about this exceptional Blackrobe so dear to the Southwest.

The design for the new statue was firmly in place, but where would the money come from to pay for the full size equestrian? Already the small maquette had created such a positive reaction, talk began to circulate about casting two large bronzes. Julián Martínez coyly lied that two would not be much more expensive than one; in truth, his generosity was incalculable.

Subsequently, a group of citizens in Tucson formed a new committee to head a project called "Three Statues for Three Centuries." If two statues would cost only slightly more than one, why not three? This time the sensitive portrayal of Kino on horseback would be cast in bronze for three places – Tucson, Magdalena, and Segno (Italy)!

Funds poured in from the City of Tucson, Pima County and several generous benefactors. But probably the most generous of all was Don Julián himself because he accepted only $25,000 for all three castings! It was as though Kino's historic generosity were being repaid in kind. The first of the three statues arrived in Tucson in May, 1988, and

Kino statue in Tucson

the statue was erected on the newly completed Kino Parkway. The second statue was completed a year later and erected in Magdalena on the toll road to Hermosillo – a decision of Donaldo Colossio, who held Kino in the highest regard. After all, every traveller in the north would see the hero who put Magdalena on the map, and, anyway, the site was close to the family ranch!

Dedication in Segno, 1991

The third statue experienced some alarming delays, but it was completed in 1990. Following masterful negotiations by Father Gomez-Padilla and Martínez, a Mexican freighter was consigned to ship the enormous bronze to Italy. Although little attention was paid to the venture, this was the first time a heroic, equestrian bronze was sculpted in the Americas and shipped to Europe! The freighter landed in Genoa, from which port the Province of Trent hauled it to the tiny town of Segno where the statue was dedicated in a jubilant celebration in June, 1991. Not even Padre

DeGrazia sketch of Kino

González could have ever dreamed of how many world dignitaries would cross the historic path of Padre Kino – for each of whom Kino held a message of hope and peace.

There is every reason to suspect that southwestern artists will not cease to reinterpret the Padre on Horseback in painting and sculpture. The unique talent of Ted de Grazia was already focused on Father Kino in 1960 in an extensive series of paintings prepared for the 250th anniversary of Kino's death. For a unique issue of *Arizona Highways*, Editor Raymond Carlson invited De Grazia to paint an historic set of twenty views of Kino's life in the Sonoran desert. Ted's sense of simplicity and anonimity, characteristically expressed in bold colors, somehow paralleled his appraisal of Padre Kino for whom he held immense esteem. One can well understand why Father Kino is the subject of art because he embodies an authentic western spirit that encompasses virility, vision, and an awesome sense of peace and purpose.

Most artists have concentrated on Kino's missions and not the man. For many decades picturesque San Xavier del Bac has been the subject of countless paintings and artistic photography. Then, in the aftermath of the discovery of Kino's grave interest flourished in the scores of surviving Jesuit missions. One Tucson artist, Ernie Cabat, repeatedly traveled with mission tour groups to capture the spirit of Mexico and the missions in water colors. Probably many others will join the ranks of Cabat and De Grazia. What the viewer will see will be a church in ruin, but the pervading presence of Padre Kino will still prevail.

One unique tribute was paid Padre Kino by the government of Mexico which issued a special stamp commemorating the 300th anniversary of his arrival in the Pimería Alta. Although strenuous efforts were made by Arizona citizens to have the U. S. Postal Service also issue a commemorative stamp, as they have done for many other pioneers, the Advisory Board vehemently denied him the privilege because they considered him unworthy, too Christian, and not sufficiently American. So Kino stands in the Hall of Statuary each day awaiting the moment when some member of Congress will wonder why this honor was never bestowed.

Arizonans and Sonorans have responded to the memory of Padre Kino in almost every way possible. Statues and paintings have been joined with song and symphony – each being composed for some phase in celebrating the continuing inspiration of this selfless missionary. Corridas were written in Sonora recalling his greatness as a vaquero; Spanish sonnets have honored his memory at village festivals. The Colegio de Kino in Hermosilllo presented a full symphony by a Mexican composer!

Nor has Kino been slighted by the media. After years of work and quiet promotion, Ken Kennedy of Phoenix, Arizona, produced *The Father Kino Story*, first as a two-hour film and later in a one-hour video. *Paths in the Wilderness* appeared as half-hour documentary, placing Kino in the context of the Sonoran desert..

Almost without question artists, authors, and producers will discover Padre Kino again and again because he was a man of the people at a time when the courage and vision of a single man could change the world for the better. He left his home in Europe to find a newer one in the Americas. And as we look back in coming to know him, we find ourselves looking forward in our own times to a future yet to be revealed, equally filled with promise and prosperity. Kino, like the desert he loved, presents us with a paradox of life itself. His legacy is more than history or art; his legacy is faith in the transforming grace of God.

A READING GUIDE FOR MISSION HISTORY

BANNON, JOHN FRANCIS, S.J. *The Spanish Borderlands Frontier, 1513-1821.* New York: Holt, Rinehart and Winston, 1970; 308 pp. One of the better studies on northern New Spain.

BOLTON, HERBERT E. *Padre on Horseback.* San Francisco: Sonora Press, 1932. Reprint, Chicago: Loyola University Press, 1963; introduction by John F. Bannon, S.J.
The Rim of Christendom. New York: Macmillan, 1936. Reprint, New York: Russell and Russell, 1960. Reprint, Tucson: University of Arizona Press, 1984. This remains the definitive biography of Eusebio Francisco Kino.

BURRUS, ERNEST J., S.J. *Kino and Manje, Explorers of Sonora and Arizona.* Rome and St. Louis: Jesuit Historical Institute, 1971. Critical text edition of the Manje diaries.
Kino and the Cartography of Northwestern New Spain. Tucson: Arizona Pioneer's Historical Society, 1965. A complete compilation of known maps by Kino.

CALARCO, DOMENICO. *L'Apostolo dei Pima: Il metodo di evangelizzazione di Eusebio Francesco Chini missionario gesuita pioniere delle Coste del Pacifico (1645-1711).* Bologna: Editrice Missionaria Italiana, 1995. A theological appraisal of Kino's mission methods.

CAVINI, VITTORIO. *L'Avventura di Kino.* Bologna: Editrice Missionaria Italiana della Coop. Sermis, 1990. Kino continues to capture the Italian mind and heart.

DONOHUE, JOHN AUGUSTINE, S. J. *After Kino: Jesuit Missions in Northwestern New Spain, 1711-1767.* Rome and St. Louis: Jesuit Historical Institute, 1969. Mostly about the Pimería Alta up to the expulsion.

ECKHART, GEORGE B. and James S. Griffith. *Temples in the Wilderness: Spanish Churches of Northern Sonora.* Tucson: Arizona Historical Society, Historical Monograph #3, 1975. Brief histories and descriptions of the major churches in the mission chain.

KENNEDY, ROGER. *Mission: The History and Architecture of the Missions of North America.* Edited by David Larkin. Boston: Houghton Mifflin. 1993. Beautiful and informative photographs with a text that presents the strength of the presence of Spanish missions in the United States.

KESSELL, JOHN L. *Mission of Sorrows: Jesuit Guevavi and the Pimas.* Tucson: The University of Arizona Press, 1970. The Pimería Alta missions as seen from the perspective of Guevavi's history.
Friars, Soldiers and Reformers: Hispanic Arizona and the Sonoran Mission Frontier, 1767-1858. Tucson: The University of Arizona Press, 1976. The Franciscan Pimería Alta as seen from the vantage point of Tumacácori mission.

KINO, EUSEBIO FRANCISCO, S. J. *Historical Memoir of the Pimería Alta.* Herbert Bolton, trans. Cleveland: Arthur Clark Co., 1919. 2 vols. Reprint: Berkeley: University of California, 1948. 2 vols. in one.
Kino's Biography of Francisco Javier Saeta. Translated and with an Epilogue by Charles W. Polzer, S. J.; original Spanish transcription edited by Ernest J. Burrus, S. J. Rome and St. Louis: Jesuit Historical Institute, 1971.
Kino's Plan for Development of the Pimería Alta. Ernest J. Burrus, S. J., trans. Tucson: Arizona Pioneer's Historical Society, 1961.
Kino Reports to Headquarters. Ernest Burrus, S. J., trans. Rome: Institutum Historicum Societatis Jesu, 1954.
Kino Writes to the Duchess. Ernest J. Burrus, S. J. trans. Rome: Institutum Historicum SocietatisJesu, 1965.

LOCKWOOD, FRANK C. *With Padre Kino on the Trail.* Tucson: The University of Arizona, 1934. Social Science Bulletin No.5. A scholar/colleague of Bolton with his own view of Kino and the missions.

MANJE, JUAN MATEO. *Luz de Tierra Incognita: Unknown Arizona and Sonora, 1693-1701.* Translated by Harry J. Karns. Tucson: Arizona Silhouettes, 1954. The diaries of Kino's trail companion.

NENTWIG, JUAN. *Rudo Ensayo: A Description of Sonora and Arizona in 1764.* Tucson: The University of Arizona Press, 1980. Translated by Albert F. Pradeau and Robert R. Rasmussen. A good historical overview; caution is urged in the botanical section.

PFEFFERKORN, IGNAZ. *Sonora: A Description of the Province.* Translated by Theodore E. Treutlein. Albuquerque: University of New Mexico Press, 1949. A classic contemporary account.

POLZER, CHARLES W., S. J. *Rules and Precepts of the Jesuit Missions of Northwestern New Spain.* Tucson: The University of Arizona Press, 1976.

PROVINCIA AUTONOMA DI TRENTO. *Padre Kino: L'avventura di Eusebio Francesco Chini, S.J (1645-1711).* Trento: Provincia di Trento, 1988. Essays on Kino in English, Italian, and Spanish from 1986 Conference.

ROCA, PAUL M. *Paths of the Padres Through Sonora.* Tucson: Arizona Historical Society, 1967. A travelog history of most Sonoran mission sites; historical accounts require critical appraisal.

SMITH, FAY JACKSON, John Kessell, and Francis Fox, S.J. *Father Kino in Arizona.* Phoenix: Arizona Historical Foundation, 1966. This book contains a more complete bibliography on Kino.

SPICER, EDWARD H *Cycles of Conquest: The Impact of Spain, Mexico and the United States on the Indians of the Southwest, 1533-1960.* Tucson: The University of Arizona Press, 1962. The classic anthropological study of the region.

WYLLYS, RUFUS KAY. *Pioneer Padre: the Life and Times of Eusebio Francisco Kino.* Dallas: Southwest Press, 1935. Not as definitive as Bolton's *Rim*, but a deserving life of Padre Kino.

WEBER, DAVID J. *The Spanish Frontier in North America.* New Haven: Yale University Press, 1992. Good background to understand the mission program; generally fair and balanced.

WOODWARD, ARTHUR, and SCOFIELD DELONG and LEFFLER MILLER. *The Missions of Northern Sonora: A 1935 Field Documentation.* Edited by Buford Pickens. Tucson: University of Arizona Press, 1993. Well illustrated and good drawings.

PHOTO CREDITS

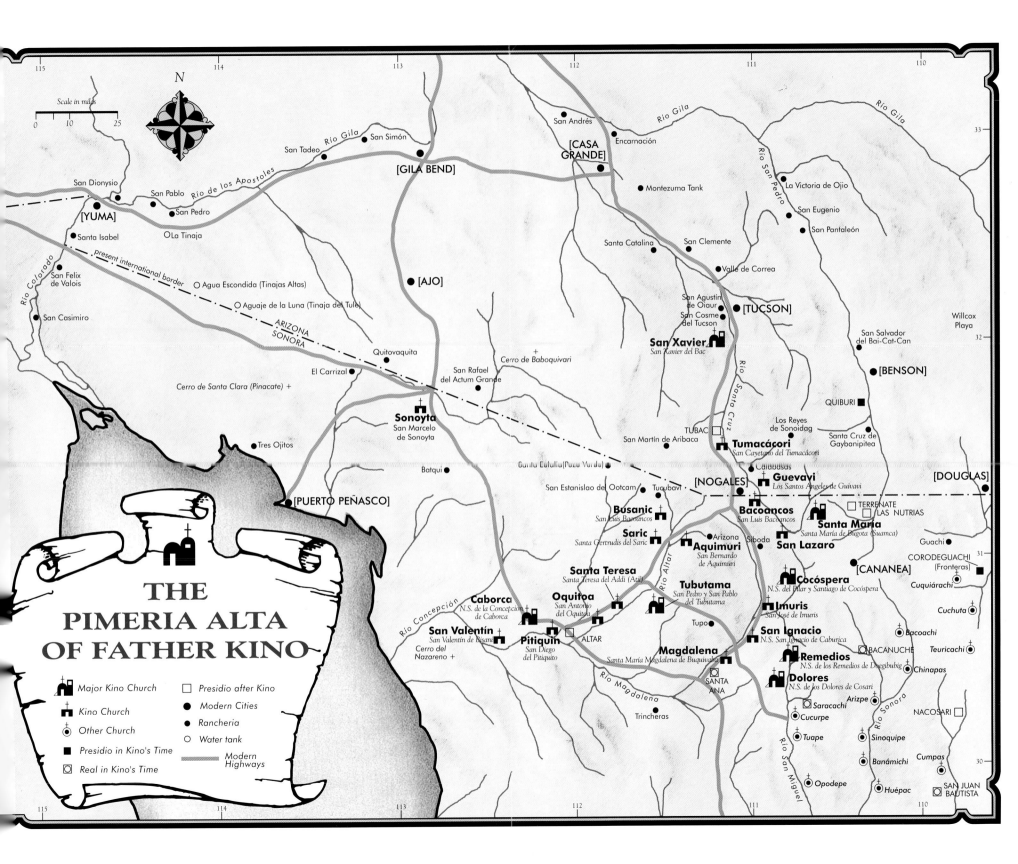